Magento 1.4 Themes Design

Customize the appearance of your Magento 1.4
e-commerce store with Magento's powerful theming
engine

Richard Carter

[PACKT] open source ✳
PUBLISHING   community experience distilled

BIRMINGHAM - MUMBAI

Magento 1.4 Themes Design

First published: January 2011

Production Reference: 1070111

Published by Packt Publishing Ltd.
32 Lincoln Road
Olton
Birmingham, B27 6PA, UK.

ISBN 978-1-849514-80-4

www.packtpub.com

Cover Image by Filippo Sarti (Filosarti@tiscali.it)

Credits

Author
Richard Carter

Reviewer
Deepak Vohra

Acquisition Editor
David Barnes

Development Editors
Tariq Rakhange

Dhiraj Chandiramani

Technical Editor
Sakina Kaydawala

Indexer
Hemangini Bari

Editorial Team Leader
Mithun Sehgal

Project Team Leader
Ashwin Shetty

Project Coordinator
Poorvi Nair

Proofreader
Linda Morris

Graphics
Nilesh Mohite

Production Coordinator
Adline Swetha Jesuthas

Cover Work
Adline Swetha Jesuthas

About the Author

Richard Carter is a frontend web developer with a passion for integrating designs in a range of open source e-commerce and content management systems, including Magento, MediaWiki, Joomla!, and Drupal. His expertise has led clients including University College Dublin, Directgov, NHS Choices, and BusinessLink (http://www.businesslink.gov.uk), to consult his knowledge on open source systems.

Richard is Creative Director at Peacock Carter Ltd (http://peacockcarter.co.uk), a web design and development agency based in the North East of England. He graduated from the University of Durham in Software Engineering, and currently lives in Newcastle-upon-Tyne. He blogs at http://www.earlgreyandbattenburg.co.uk/ and tweets at http://twitter.com/RichardCarter.

Magento 1.4 Theme Design is the author's fourth book: Richard has previously written *MediaWiki Skins Design*, *Magento 1.3 Theme Design*, and *Joomla! 1.5 Templates Cookbook*, and has acted as a technical reviewer on *MediaWiki 1.1 Beginners Guide* and *Inkscape Illustrator's Guide*.

Thanks to Magento for creating such a versatile e-commerce system — this book wouldn't exist without it — and for those who took the time to review *Magento 1.3 Theme Design*, as your comments were valuable in updating the content for this book.

Thanks are also due to my family and friends, whose constant support has proved both useful and welcome. In particular, my thanks are due to EJ and, of course, Alexandra, who have put up with months of inane mumbling and cursing at the screen!

About the Reviewer

Deepak Vohra is a consultant and a principal member of the http://nubean.com software company. Deepak is a Sun Certified Java Programmer and Web Component Developer, and has worked in the fields of XML and Java programming, and J2EE for over five years. Deepak is the co-author of the Apress book–*Pro XML Development with Java Technology* and was the technical reviewer for the O'Reilly book–*WebLogic: The Definitive Guide*. Deepak was also the technical reviewer for the Course Technology PTR book–*Ruby Programming for the Absolute Beginner*, and the technical editor for the Manning Publications book–*Prototype and Scriptaculous in Action*. Deepak is also the author of the Packt Publishing books–*JDBC 4.0 and Oracle JDeveloper for J2EE Development* and *Processing XML Documents with Oracle JDeveloper 11g*.

www.PacktPub.com

Support files, e-books, discount offers, and more

You might want to visit www.PacktPub.com for support files and downloads related to your book.

Did you know that Packt offers e-book versions of every book published, with PDF and e-Pub files available? You can upgrade to the e-book version at www.PacktPub.com and as a print book customer, you are entitled to a discount on the e-book copy. Get in touch with us at service@packtpub.com for more details.

At www.PacktPub.com, you can also read a collection of free technical articles, sign up for a range of free newsletters and receive exclusive discounts and offers on Packt books and e-books.

http://PacktLib.PacktPub.com

Do you need instant solutions to your IT questions? PacktLib is Packt's online digital book library. Here, you can access, read, and search across Packt's entire library of books.

Why Subscribe?
- Fully searchable across every book published by Packt
- Copy and paste, print and bookmark content
- On demand and accessible via web browser

Free Access for Packt account holders

If you have an account with Packt at www.PacktPub.com, you can use this to access PacktLib today and view nine entirely free books. Simply use your login credentials for immediate access.

Table of Contents

Preface

Magento is a popular open source e-commerce project. While it comes with a number of 'default' themes to change the look and feel of your store, many people both new and old to Magento struggle with even the more basic aspects of customizing Magento themes. When you read this book you'll see how to change the basics of your Magento theme, create a new custom theme, and much more.

The book is a step-by-step guide to theming Magento, aimed at readers with little technical expertise.

In short, the book guides the common aspects of theming and customizing Magento 1.4 and an equally useful step-by-step walkthrough of integrating more unusual items into your Magento store.

What this book covers

Chapter 1, Introduction to Magento, introduces Magento, including the installation of the software and avoiding common pitfalls in this process. This chapter is an invaluable guide for those who are new to everything in Magento, or just those who are new to Magento 1.4.

Chapter 2, Exploring Magento Themes, introduces theming in the context of Magento and covers terminology used within the Magento project that relates to Magento in a wider context—from interfaces to packages—and more specifically, theme terminology, from skins to layouts, and template files.

Chapter 3, Magento Theme Basics, covers the basics of Magento theming, from changing your store's color scheme to updating your store's logo. This chapter concentrates on altering existing Magento themes to achieve the theming aims for your store.

Chapter 4, Magento Theme Layouts, provides an overview of what a layout is in the context of the Magento system, related terminology including layout handles and layout actions, and uses a number of useful step-by-step guides to common tasks you may need to use within Magento to create your theme.

Chapter 5, Non-default Magento Themes, covers the building blocks of creating your own Magento 1.4 theme, from replicating the necessary file hierarchy for your theme to enabling your new theme, styling your store's search feature, and altering your store's footer area.

Chapter 6, More Magento Theming, built on the previous chapter's content, from integrating `@font-face` fonts into your Magento store for higher-fidelity typography in your Magento store to customizing your store's navigation.

Chapter 7, Customizing Advanced Magento Layout, looks into more advanced customization and manipulation of Magento layout in order to customize your Magento store.

Chapter 8, Magento E-mail Templates, looks at customizing e-mail templates that are used to contact customers during key processes of their interaction with your Magento store, as well as integrating the well-known e-mail newsletter system-CampaignMonitor.

Chapter 9, Social Media and Magento, guides you through integrating popular social media websites—Twitter and Facebook—with your Magento store, from adding a Facebook **Like** button to your store to adding your latest tweets to your Magento store.

Chapter 10, Magento Print Style, sees you creating a custom print stylesheet to better allow your store's customers to print key pages from your store.

What you need for this book

You will need version 1.4 of Magento Community Edition or the equivalent version of the Enterprise or Professional editions. A familiarity with CSS and (X)HTML is recommended, and knowledge of PHP is beneficial.

Who this book is for

This book is aimed at web designers and web developers who are not familiar with Magento at all and to Magento designers and developers who are more familiar with Magento 1.3 than Magento 1.4. The book assumes knowledge of HTML and CSS and an awareness, but not in-depth knowledge of PHP syntax.

Conventions

In this book, you will find a number of styles of text that distinguish between different kinds of information. Here are some examples of these styles, and an explanation of their meaning.

Code words in text are shown as follows: " The default layout for the checkout view is defined in the `checkout.xml` file in the `app/design/frontend/base/default/layout` directory."

A block of code is set as follows:

```
<action method="setTemplate">
<template>page/2columns-left.phtml</template>
</action>
```

When we wish to draw your attention to a particular part of a code block, the relevant lines or items are set in bold:

```
<reference name="left">
 <block type="core/template" name="left.permanent.callout"
template="callouts/left_col.phtml" />
</reference>
```

New terms and **important words** are shown in bold. Words that you see on the screen, in menus or dialog boxes for example, appear in the text like this: " Uncheck the checkbox next to **Add Block Names to Hints** and select **Yes** from the drop-down field ".

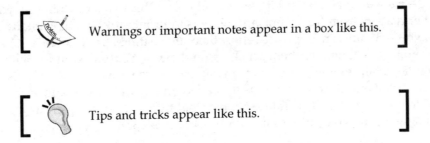

Warnings or important notes appear in a box like this.

Tips and tricks appear like this.

Reader feedback

Feedback from our readers is always welcome. Let us know what you think about this book—what you liked or may have disliked. Reader feedback is important for us to develop titles that you really get the most out of.

To send us general feedback, simply send an e-mail to `feedback@packtpub.com`, and mention the book title via the subject of your message.

If there is a book that you need and would like to see us publish, please send us a note in the **SUGGEST A TITLE** form on `www.packtpub.com` or e-mail `suggest@packtpub.com`.

If there is a topic that you have expertise in and you are interested in either writing or contributing to a book, see our author guide on `www.packtpub.com/authors`.

Customer support

Now that you are the proud owner of a Packt book, we have a number of things to help you to get the most from your purchase.

Downloading the example code for this book

You can download the example code files for all Packt books you have purchased from your account at `http://www.PacktPub.com`. If you purchased this book elsewhere, you can visit `http://www.PacktPub.com/support` and register to have the files e-mailed directly to you.

Errata

Although we have taken every care to ensure the accuracy of our content, mistakes do happen. If you find a mistake in one of our books—maybe a mistake in the text or the code—we would be grateful if you would report this to us. By doing so, you can save other readers from frustration and help us improve subsequent versions of this book. If you find any errata, please report them by visiting `http://www.packtpub.com/support`, selecting your book, clicking on the **errata submission form** link, and entering the details of your errata. Once your errata are verified, your submission will be accepted and the errata will be uploaded on our website, or added to any list of existing errata, under the Errata section of that title. Any existing errata can be viewed by selecting your title from `http://www.packtpub.com/support`.

Piracy

Piracy of copyright material on the Internet is an ongoing problem across all media. At Packt, we take the protection of our copyright and licenses very seriously. If you come across any illegal copies of our works, in any form, on the Internet, please provide us with the location address or website name immediately so that we can pursue a remedy.

Please contact us at copyright@packtpub.com with a link to the suspected pirated material.

We appreciate your help in protecting our authors, and our ability to bring you valuable content.

Questions

You can contact us at questions@packtpub.com if you are having a problem with any aspect of the book, and we will do our best to address it.

1
Introduction to Magento

The Internet is an important sector of many businesses, both large and small, in the modern world; it's now rare for a company to not have at least a basic web presence and increasingly unlikely that a company's products are not sold online. Magento is a powerful e-commerce system, used by international organizations such as Homedics, The North Face, Samsung, and 3M.

In this chapter, you will see the following:

- Take a look at what Magento is and what Magento can do
- Discover the differences between Magento 1.3 and Magento 1.4
- See the default themes that come installed with Magento 1.4
- Look at a showcase of custom Magento themes from real websites
- Find out the particular challenges in customizing Magento themes
- Install and configure Magento 1.4 ready for theming

As you will come to see, Magento is quite a large e-commerce system and this book will guide you through customizing its quirks and eccentricities.

What is Magento?

Magento Commerce (`http://www.magentocommerce.com`) is an open source e-commerce framework: simply, it's a free to use and modify way to start selling products online.

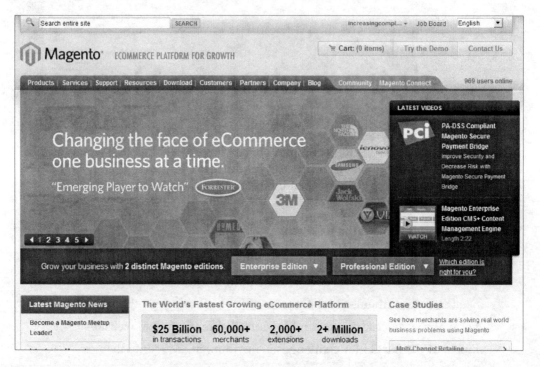

Magento is written in the PHP programming language using an object-orientated architecture, allowing features such as additional payment gateways, integration with social networks such as Twitter and Facebook, and customization for different product types to be easily added.

The default installation of Magento provides a huge number of e-commerce and related features, supports multiple stores being managed from the same control panel, and—importantly for us—provides the ability for very heavily customized themes. The system has been criticized for being slow to load, which can be at least partially mitigated with the use of built-in caches.

Magento's features

As with other e-commerce systems, Magento allows products to be added, edited, manipulated, and organized within categories. You are able to control your products' names, descriptions, prices, and upload multiple photographs for each product in your store. Magento also lets you create variations of products in your store, so you can have one product which is available in multiple colors (such as blue, red, and black) within Magento. In other e-commerce systems, you may have to add the blue, red, and black products as three separate products.

In addition to these 'standard' e-commerce features, Magento also has provisions to perform the following:

- Manage both the sending of e-mail newsletters and the managing of subscribers to these lists
- Manage non-product pages through its content management system (CMS)
- Organize polls of your store's visitors

Additional features are available in the other versions of Magento; Magento Enterprise Edition and Magento Professional Edition, but this book concentrates on Magento Community Edition and everything in this book can be applied to all editions of Magento.

Differences between Magento 1.3 and Magento 1.4 themes

There are some fairly major changes between Magento 1.3 and Magento 1.4. Magento 1.4 fixes some known bugs and adds new features, some of which had to be added as separate modules in Magento 1.3, including the use of canonical URLs.

It is not only the features of Magento that vary between versions 1.3 and 1.4, although the structure of themes has changed quite significantly. In particular, the way theme hierarchy works in Magento 1.4 has been changed to allow greater modularity between themes. That is, the new theme hierarchy in Magento means that there should always be *some* styling to elements in your theme if you forget to style them.

In addition to this, default classes and ids used in Magento 1.3 have been changed in Magento 1.4 and the `.phtml` templates, that a Magento theme is comprised of, have been changed to provide improved accessibility in places, or just to better accommodate new or changed functionality. In particular, `alt` and `title` attributes have been added to the markup and HTML has been validated throughout the template blocks.

As such, porting a Magento 1.3 theme to Magento 1.4 is likely to be a very tedious task, and you may well be better off starting the theme from scratch.

Default Magento 1.4 themes

By default, Magento comes with three different themes:

- Default
- Modern
- Blue

You can easily preview these themes on the Magento demonstration site at `http://demo.magentocommerce.com`, and by selecting an option from the **Select Store** drop-down box located in the footer of the site (**Main Store** displays Magento's default theme):

Magento Default theme

The Default theme is what you see when you install Magento 1.4. The homepage is based upon a three column structure:

In the preceding screenshot, you can see the distinction between each column with the central column being used for content and the side columns being used for additional information such as the **shopping cart**, product tags, and advertisements for products within your store.

Product pages display a prominent picture of the product in a two column layout:

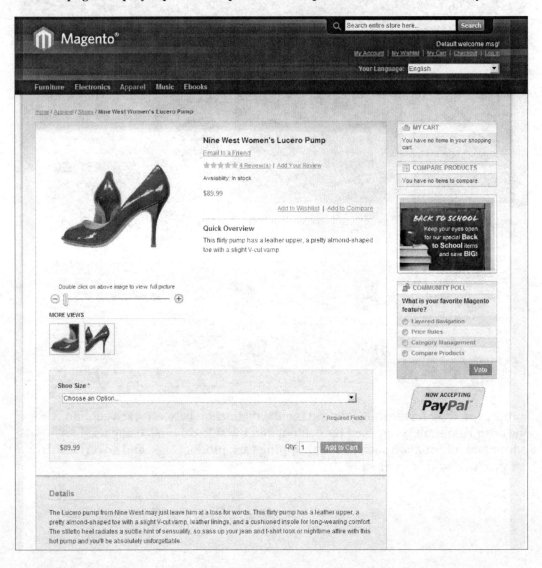

On the product page, you can see Magento adds a breadcrumb trail to where the page is located within your store's hierarchy, as well as including multiple photographs of the product which can be enlarged.

Finally, each product category page reverts to the three column structure of the homepage:

The category page reverts to a three column layout, presenting products as a grid by default. As it is common across many Magento themes, you're able to view products in two distinct ways: **Grid** view displays products in a grid:

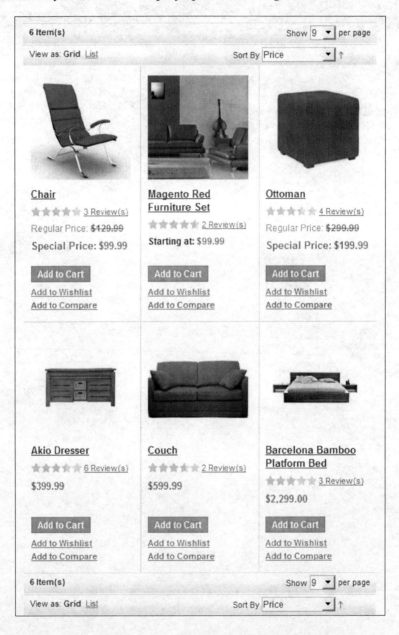

List view allows for more information about products to be displayed alongside the product photograph and other information shown in the grid view:

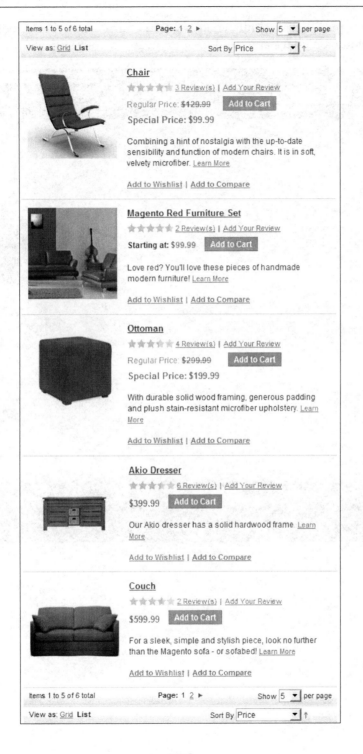

Items 1 to 5 of 6 total   Page: 1 2 ▶   Show 5 ▼ per page

View as: Grid List   Sort By Price ▼ ↑

Chair
★★★★☆ 3 Review(s) | Add Your Review

Regular Price: ~~$129.99~~   [Add to Cart]

Special Price: $99.99

Combining a hint of nostalgia with the up-to-date sensibility and function of modern chairs. It is in soft, velvety microfiber. Learn More

Add to Wishlist | Add to Compare

Magento Red Furniture Set
★★★★★ 2 Review(s) | Add Your Review

Starting at: $99.99   [Add to Cart]

Love red? You'll love these pieces of handmade modern furniture! Learn More

Add to Wishlist | Add to Compare

Ottoman
★★★☆☆ 4 Review(s) | Add Your Review

Regular Price: ~~$299.99~~   [Add to Cart]

Special Price: $199.99

With durable solid wood framing, generous padding and plush stain-resistant microfiber upholstery. Learn More

Add to Wishlist | Add to Compare

Akio Dresser
★★★☆☆ 6 Review(s) | Add Your Review

$399.99   [Add to Cart]

Our Akio dresser has a solid hardwood frame. Learn More

Add to Wishlist | Add to Compare

Couch
★★★★☆ 2 Review(s) | Add Your Review

$599.99   [Add to Cart]

For a sleek, simple and stylish piece, look no further than the Magento sofa - or sofabed! Learn More

Add to Wishlist | Add to Compare

Items 1 to 5 of 6 total   Page: 1 2 ▶   Show 5 ▼ per page

View as: Grid List   Sort By Price ▼ ↑

Once you have installed Magento, you'll see that your Default theme looks a little different as you won't have any products or content in your store yet:

Modern theme

The Modern theme also comes with the default Magento installation and presents a more modern, clean design for your store, with space for a large splash image to advertise a particular seasonal product or offer:

The product category page is much less cluttered than in the Default theme and uses a two column layout, with the familiar **Grid** and **List** views for products in the store:

The Modern theme's product page follows a similar layout to the category view:

Blue theme

Magento's Blue theme is based upon the Default theme, with a slightly cleaner look than the Default theme:

Showcase of Magento themes

There are a plethora of e-commerce websites that make use of Magento and some of them truly demonstrate how flexible Magento can be when it comes to theming. Here is a selection of live Magento stores that really push the platform beyond the typical Magento themes you've already seen:

Harvey Nichols

Harvey Nichols is an upmarket department store with stores across the UK. Their Magento store (`http://www.harveynichols.com`) reflects the position in the market and presents images their customers would be familiar with:

As you can see, the store's homepage is heavily styled away from the default themes available in Magento and with their primary category navigation displayed to the top-right of the screen, it makes these highly visible to customers.

When interacted with, the store's category view expands to display more specific sub-categories:

The product detail view is also heavily customized, with information on the product, delivery, and size guides all provided with their own separate blocks:

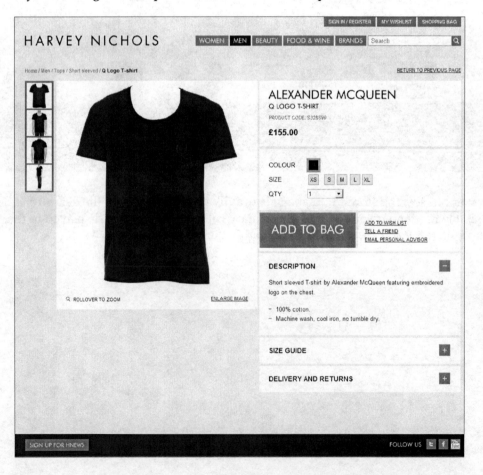

Mark One

Mark One (`http://www.mk1.co.nz`) is a New Zealand based graphic novel and comic book specialist:

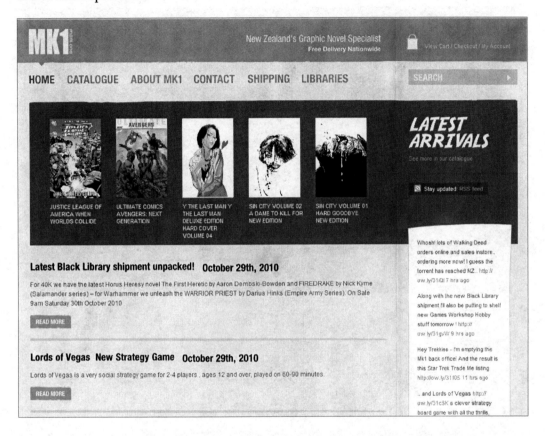

As you can see, the homepage is quite heavily customized, with the latest products displayed across the top of the page and the store's latest news listed beneath. The homepage is actually based on the WordPress blogging platform with the relevant data pulled from Magento.

The product detail page, which is part of the Magento store, is similarly styled in an appealing way, with plenty of screen space given to information about the product and related products being listed beneath:

Zhu Zhu

Zhu Zhu (http://www.zhu-zhu.co.uk) is a 'natural well-being' store based in the UK. The homepage is quite graphically intriguing and appealing to the store's likely customers:

The footer makes good use of static blocks in Magento (you'll discover more about these in a later chapter) to tell customers about the store, delivery, and payment options available to them:

The product detail view also heavily customizes Magento: note the customized graphics for the 'zoom in' bar for product photographs:

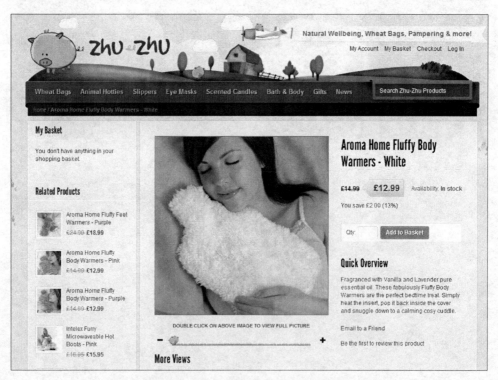

Challenges of Magento theme design

Magento is a comprehensive and at times, a complex system, and this is reflected in some of the challenges that designers come across in creating themes for Magento:

- Complexity: as Magento is a large system, it can initially be infuriating to theme for, though after some time you should become more familiar with Magento's inner workings
- Breadth of knowledge: Magento theming involves tackling a mixture of XML (for layout files), CSS (for style), (X)HTML and snippets of PHP (for the templates)
- Lack of documentation: while the Magento community is large and still growing, you may find that many of the help documents on the Magento website are a version more out-of-date or offer inadequate help

Why create a custom Magento theme?

There are a number of reasons you would want to create or customize a Magento theme:

- The first and most obvious reason to customize your Magento theme is that this can help you to distinguish your store from your competitors.
- Customizing your Magento theme can also allow you to better integrate extensions from Magento Connect in to your store, with additional features.
- If you have an existing website and wish to add e-commerce by integrating Magento around the existing system, theming Magento can make sure that there is a visually seamless integration between the two systems.
- Theming Magento can also be useful to customize your store to reflect different expectations of your customers from around the world. For example, customers in some countries may expect components of your store to appear in one location on their screen, so you could theme Magento to reflect this if your customers are primarily from that country.

Installing Magento 1.4

Before we get started with customizing the look and feel of our Magento store, you will need to install Magento 1.4.

Pre-installation check: magento-check.php

If you're not sure if Magento will be supported by your hosting platform, you can try running the Magento Check utility available from the Magento website at `http://www.magentocommerce.com/knowledge-base/entry/how-do-i-know-if-my-server-is-compatible-with-magento`:

 Using the utility is much quicker than attempting to upload and install Magento, so it's worth trying if you're unsure!

Extract the `magento-check.php` file if necessary and upload it to the server you wish to run Magento on (for example, `example.com/magento/magento-check.php`). Use your browser to visit the file; you should see this if your server is able to support Magento 1.4:

Congratulations! Your server meets the requirements for Magento.

- You have **PHP 5.2.0** (or greater)
- Safe Mode is **off**
- You have **MySQL 4.1.20** (or greater)
- You have the **curl** extension
- You have the **dom** extension
- You have the **gd** extension
- You have the **hash** extension
- You have the **iconv** extension
- You have the **mcrypt** extension
- You have the **pcre** extension
- You have the **pdo** extension
- You have the **pdo_mysql** extension
- You have the **simplexml** extension

If the Magento Check tool tells you that you're unable to use Magento on your server, the Magento Check tool lists any requirements it has that are not met, such as in the following example:

Your server does not meet the following requirements in order to install Magento.
The following requirements failed, please contact your hosting provider in order to receive assistance with meeting the system requirements for Magento:

- You need **MySQL 4.1.20** (or greater)

The following requirements were successfully met:

- You have **PHP 5.2.0** (or greater)
- Safe Mode is **off**
- You have the **curl** extension
- You have the **dom** extension
- You have the **gd** extension
- You have the **hash** extension
- You have the **iconv** extension
- You have the **mcrypt** extension
- You have the **pcre** extension
- You have the **pdo** extension
- You have the **pdo_mysql** extension
- You have the **simplexml** extension

Downloading Magento 1.4 Community Edition

To download Magento 1.4, go to the Magento Commerce website at `http://www.magentocommerce.com/download` and click on the **Download** button corresponding to the latest version of Magento Community Edition after picking your desired download format (`.zip`, `.tar.gz`, or `.tar.bz2`):

Save this file to your computer and extract it from its compressed format. You can then upload the Magento files to your server using FTP.

Be patient

Uploading the files to your server can take some time as there are a lot of them—Magento is a complex package!

Installing and configuring Magento

Once this is done, visit your Magento installation's directory (for example, `example.com/magento`) and you should be redirected to the Magento installation wizard (say, `example.com/magento/index.php/install`), where you'll be presented with a license agreement:

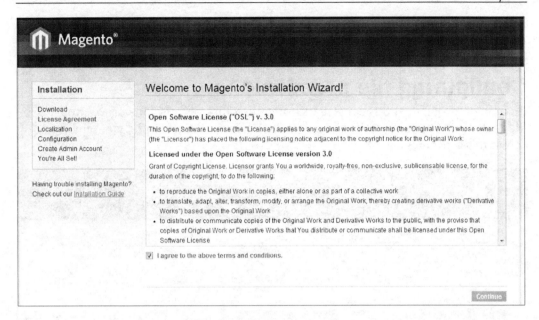

To continue the installation, read through the agreement and then check **I agree to the above terms and conditions** (assuming, of course, that you do agree). Once you click on the **Continue** button, you'll need to configure the **Localization** settings:

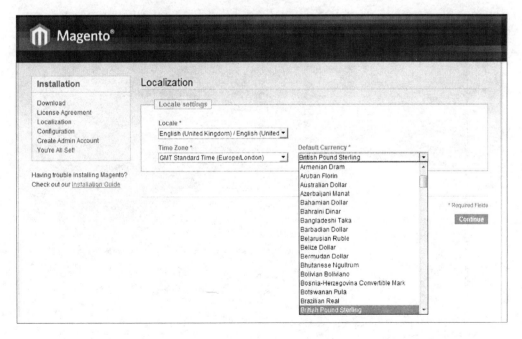

Select your **Locale**, **Time Zone**, and **Default Currency**—by default these are set to American values—and then click on the **Continue** button.

Configuring file permissions

A common problem at this stage is incorrect directory permissions preventing Magento from changing settings on your installation. For example, you may come across this error message:

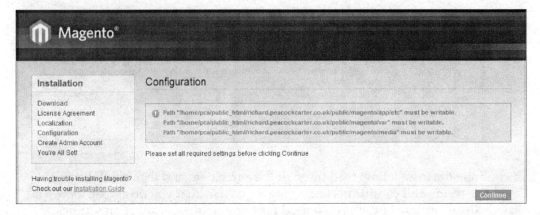

To change file permissions, you can usually right-click on a particular directory on your server within your FTP program:

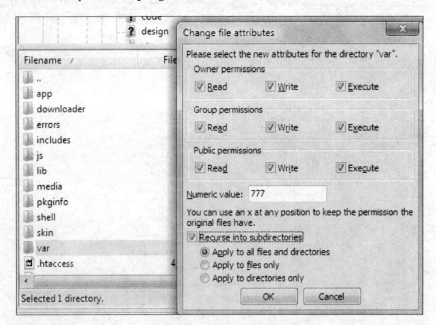

Be sure to apply the new file permissions to files and other directories within the directories. As in this example, the common directories that need their permissions changed in order to fully install Magento are:

- `/app/etc`
- `/media`
- `/var`

Configuring Magento

Next, you will need to configure the database and other settings for your Magento installation, which are split in to three steps:

- **Database Connection**
- **Web access options**
- **Session Storage Options**

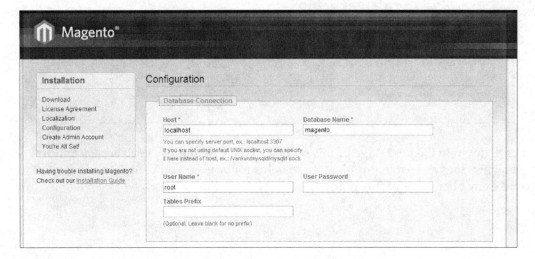

Some of the fields here—**Host**, **Database Name**, and **User Name**—are already populated, but you may need to change these. You will probably need to provide a password for the database under **User Password**.

Tables Prefix

The **Tables Prefix** field allows you to get Magento to add a common phrase before each table's name in your database. This is particularly useful if you're installing Magento in a database with other existing software such as Wordpress or Drupal. An example value you could use here might be magento_, which would rename a table called users to magento_users in your database.

Scroll down to the next stage of this section of the installation, **Web access options**. Magento does its best to populate these fields for you, so you probably won't need to make any alterations at this point:

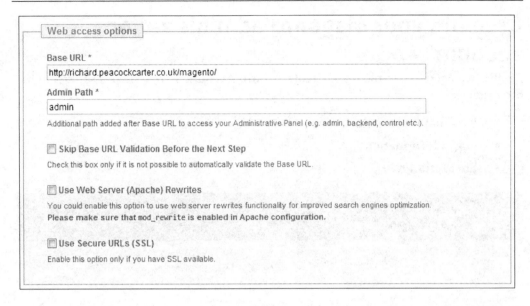

The **Base URL** field is the location of your Magento installation; the **Admin Path** field tells Magento where to locate your administrator panel. By default, this field's value is set to **admin**, meaning that if you had installed Magento at example.com/ magento, your administration panel would be reached at example.com/magento/ admin.

The final step at this stage of the installation is to set the **Session Storage Options**; by default the value of the **Save Session Data In** field is set to **File System**; that is how we'll leave it:

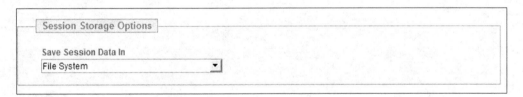

You can now click on the **Continue** button to progress to the next stage of your Magento installation: the creation of your Magento administrator account.

Creating your Magento administration account

Finally, we need to complete the **Create Admin Account** step, which is broken in to three stages:

- **Personal Information**
- **Login Information**
- **Encryption Key**

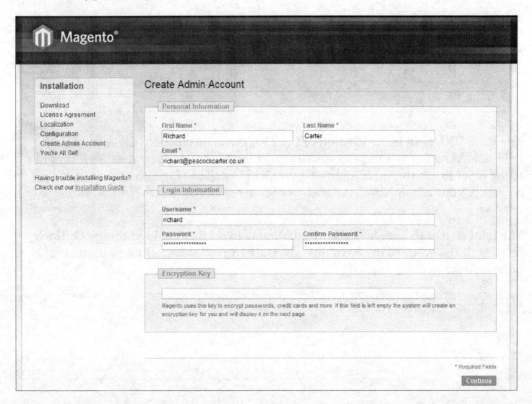

The **Personal Information** stage requires you to enter your **First Name**, **Last Name** as well as your e-mail address (**Email**). All of these fields are required, so you won't be able to complete installation of Magento without entering values in them.

You need to fill in the **Login Information** section next: this creates your **Username** which you can use to log in to your Magento installation.

Password requirements

The password you chose at this stage must be at least 7 characters long and contain a mix of numbers and letters to be accepted by the Magento installation wizard.

The last step is to set an **Encryption Key** if you want to set a custom one. Magento uses the encryption key to help secure information in your store such as credit card numbers and passwords, so it's worth making it as obscure as possible and remembering not to share your encryption key for Magento with anyone else. If you don't enter a custom encryption key, Magento will generate one for you, which is displayed on the subsequent screen once you have completed the **Create Admin Account** step of installation and clicked on **Continue**:

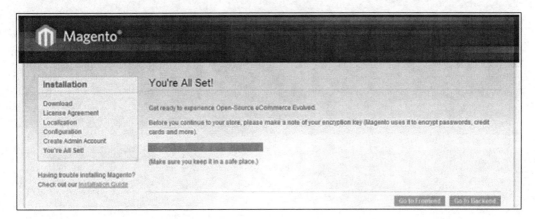

Summary

You've now seen what Magento can do, and the changes and improvements in this newer version of Magento. Perhaps more importantly, we've installed Magento too, so it's ready to start theming! The remainder of this book covers customizing your Magento theme, from the basics such as changing your store's logos and color schemes to e-mail templates, and more.

2
Exploring Magento Themes

As you've already seen, Magento can be a complex platform to customize, so this chapter will help you to explore Magento themes, including the following:

- Magento terminology
- What a Magento theme is: the elements that comprise a Magento theme
- Theme hierarchy in Magento
- Magento's Blank theme
- Installing and activating a Magento theme

Magento terminology

Before you look at Magento themes, it's beneficial to know the difference between what Magento calls **interfaces** and what Magento calls **themes**, and the distinguishing factors of **websites** and **stores**.

Magento websites and Magento stores

To add to this, the terms websites and stores have a slightly different meaning in Magento than in general and in other systems. For example, if your business is called M2, you might have three Magento stores (managed through the same installation of Magento) called:

- Blue Store
- Red Store
- Yellow Store

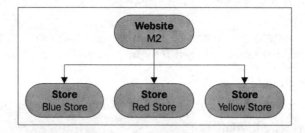

In this case, Magento refers to M2 as the website and the stores are Blue Store, Red Store, and Yellow Store. Each store then has one or more **store views** associated with it too. The simplest Magento website consists of a store and store view (usually of the same name):

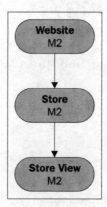

A slightly more complex Magento store may just have one store view for each store. This is a useful technique if you want to manage more than one store in the same Magento installation, with each store selling different products (for example, the Blue Store sells blue products and the Yellow Store sells yellow products).

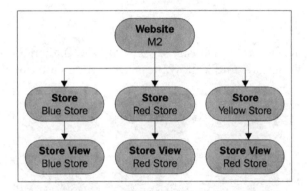

If a store were to make use of more than one Magento store view, it might be, to present customers with a bi-lingual website. For example, our Blue Store may have an English, French, and Japanese store view associated with it:

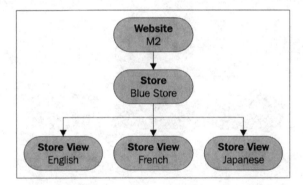

Magento interfaces

An interface consists of one or more Magento themes that comprise how your stores look and function for your customers. Interfaces can be assigned at two levels in Magento:

- At the website level
- At the store view level

If you assign an interface at the website level of your Magento installation, all stores associated with the interface inherit the interface. For example, imagine your website is known as M2 in Magento and it contains three stores called:

- Blue Store
- Red Store
- Yellow Store

If you assign an interface at the website level (that is, M2), then the subsequent stores, Blue Store, Red Store, and Yellow Store, inherit this interface:

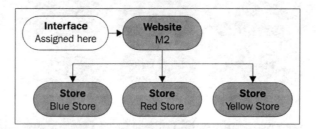

If you assigned the interface at the store view level of Magento, then each store view can retain a different interface:

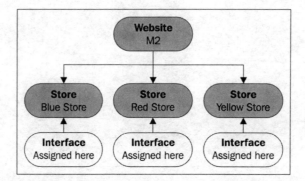

Magento packages

A Magento package typically contains a base theme, which contains all of the templates, and other files that Magento needs to run successfully, and a custom theme.

Let's take a typical example of a Magento store, M2. This may have two packages: the base package, located in the `app/design/frontend/base/` directory and another package which itself consists of two themes:

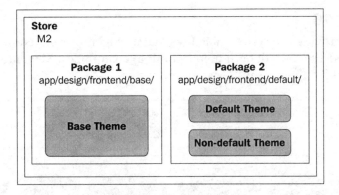

The base theme is in the `app/design/frontend/base/` directory. The second package contains the custom theme's default theme in the `app/design/frontend/default/` directory, which acts as a base theme within the package. The custom theme itself, which is the non-default theme, is in the `app/design/frontend/our-custom-theme/default/` and `app/design/frontend/our-custom-theme/custom-theme/` directories.

By default, Magento will look for a required file in the following order:

1. Custom theme directory: `app/design/frontend/our-custom-theme/custom-theme/`

2. Custom theme's default directory: `app/design/frontend/our-custom-theme/default/`

3. Base directory: `app/design/frontend/base/`

Magento themes

A Magento theme fits in to the Magento hierarchy in a number of positions: it can act as an interface or as a store view. There's more to discover about Magento themes yet, though there are two types of Magento theme: a **base theme** (this was called a **default theme** in Magento 1.3) and a **non-default theme**.

Base theme

A base theme provides all conceivable files that a Magento store requires to run without error, so that non-default themes built to customize a Magento store will not cause errors if a file does not exist within it.

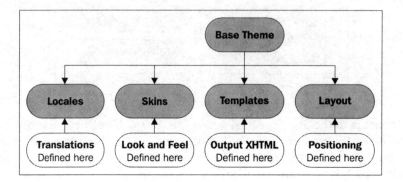

The base theme does not contain all of the CSS and images required to style your store, as you'll be doing this with our non-default theme.

Don't change the base package!

It is important that you do not edit any files in the base package and that you do not attempt to create a custom theme in the base package, as this will make upgrading Magento fully difficult. Make sure any custom themes you are working on are within their own design package; for example, your theme's files should be located at `app/design/frontend/your-package-name/default` and `skin/frontend/your-package-name/default`.

Default themes

A default theme in Magento 1.4 changes aspects of your store but does not need to include every file required by Magento as a base theme does, though it must just contain at least one file for at least one aspect of a theme (that is, locales, skins, templates, layout):

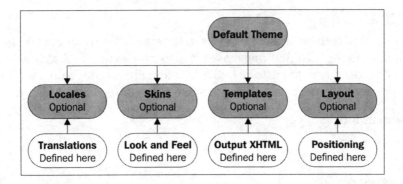

Default themes in Magento 1.3

In Magento 1.3, the default theme acted the way the base theme did in Magento 1.4, providing every file that your Magento store required to operate.

Non-default themes

A non-default theme changes aspects of a Magento store but does not need to include every file required by Magento as the base theme does; it must just contain at least one file for at least one aspect of a theme (that is, locales, skins, templates, layout):

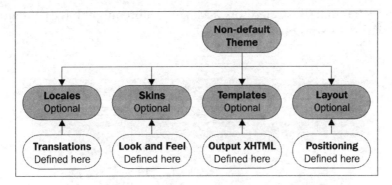

In this way, non-default themes are similar to a default theme in Magento. Non-default themes can be used to alter your Magento store for different seasonal events such as Christmas, Easter, Eid, Passover, and other religious festivals, as well as events in your industry's corporate calendar such as annual exhibitions and conferences.

Blocks in Magento

Magento uses **blocks** to differentiate between the various components of its functionality, with the idea that this makes it easier for Magento developers and Magento theme designers to customize the functionality of Magento and the look and feel of Magento respectively. There are two types of blocks in Magento:

- **Content blocks**
- **Structural blocks**

Content blocks

A content block displays the generated XHTML provided by Magento for any given feature. Content blocks are used *within* Magento structural blocks. Examples of content blocks in Magento include the following:

- The search feature
- Product listings
- The mini cart
- Category listings
- Site navigation links
- Callouts (advertising blocks)

The following diagram illustrates how a Magento store might have content blocks positioned within its structural blocks:

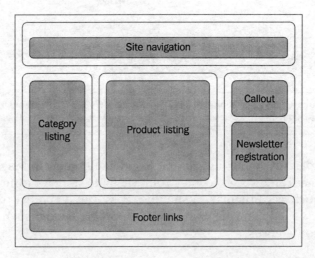

Simply, content blocks are the *what* of a Magento theme: they define what type of content appears within any given page or view within Magento.

Structural blocks

In Magento, a structural block exists only to maintain a visual hierarchy to a page. Typical structural blocks in a Magento theme include:

- Header
- Primary area
- Left column
- Right column
- Footer

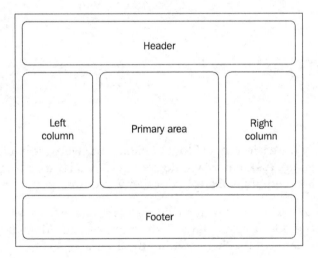

What makes a Magento theme?

A Magento theme is a collection of files that define the look, layout, and other outputs from the Magento system.

Unique aspects of a Magento theme

Magento themes differ from design implementations in other content management systems and e-commerce platforms in a few key ways:

1. Maximum ability to customize Magento
2. Support for multiple concurrent themes

3. They offer an uninterrupted workflow
4. They minimize debugging time for errors

Magento's theming system provides the ability to highly customize the way Magento looks to your customers: you can customize every aspect of your Magento store through layout, skin files (CSS and images), templates, and locale files.

The support of multiple concurrent themes is another feature which makes Magento somewhat unique in its field, allowing you to style your store differently for Magento.

Typical Magento theme file types

The files in a Magento theme can be categorized into a few categories:

- Skins
- Layouts
- Templates
- Locales

Skins

Skins are probably the easiest aspect to understand for web designers who are not familiar with Magento. A skin in Magento consists of CSS (Cascading Style Sheets), images, and any behavioral JavaScript your theme requires.

Skins are located in the `/skin/frontend/interface-name/theme-name` directory in Magento 1.4, where `interface-name` is the name of your Magento interface, and `theme-name` is the name of the theme within the interface.

Magento 1.3 skin directory

In Magento 1.3, a theme's skin directory was something like `app/design/frontend/default`.

Layouts

Layouts define the structure of blocks for different pages in your Magento store in XML (`.xml`) files. A theme's layout files are located in the `app/design/frontend/interface-name/theme-name/layout/` directory (the same as Magento 1.3).

Layout files can also define meta information for pages and which character set a page should be encoded in (for example, utf-8).

Templates

Templates are used in Magento themes to generate any necessary (X)HTML mark-up for the various content blocks in your store such as the basket, category links, and product view. They use a mixture of (X)HTML and PHP and are saved as .phtml files. You will find a theme's template files in the app/design/frontend/ interface-name/theme-name/template/ directory of your Magento installation.

Locales

Locales are possibly the least-common element of Magento theming; a locale is used to customize the language of a Magento store. For example a locale might translate store elements to Spanish for a store with a Spanish store view.

Locales are stored in the app/design/frontend/interface-name/theme-name/ locale/ directory relative to where you installed Magento, which is where they were also located in Magento 1.3. Locale files are stored as plain text files such as .csv (*comma-separated variable* format).

Theme hierarchy in Magento: the fallback pattern

Magento has rules in place to tell it which files have precedence to be displayed if there are multiple themes active on a store.

Theme hierarchy exists in Magento to ensure that, if a file (for example, a stylesheet or a template) does not exist in a customized theme, Magento will still be able to find the file in the base theme. This is known as the fallback theme.

The base theme

Magento theme hierarchies worked differently in Magento 1.3: there was no base theme in Magento, which meant it was easy to forget to add a required file to your store's default Magento theme, potentially meaning that your store could break when viewed by visitors.

The addition of the base theme in Magento 1.4 onwards should negate this problem, so long as you build your theme correctly, creating only files you have changed to customize your new theme, and not duplicating an existing theme, as these were the common practices in Magento 1.3.

An example of theme hierarchy

Take the example of a Magento store, M2. At the very top of the hierarchy is your custom theme.

If this theme requests a file—use a stylesheet, `style.css`, as an example—Magento will first look in `app/design/frontend/your-custom-package/your-custom-theme`, and then `skin/frontend/your-custom-package/your-custom-theme`. If `style.css` can't be found in these directories, Magento will resort to the next theme in the hierarchy; your custom package's default theme. This means Magento next looks for the file in the `app/design/frontend/your-custom-package/default` and `skin/frontend-your-custom-package/default`:

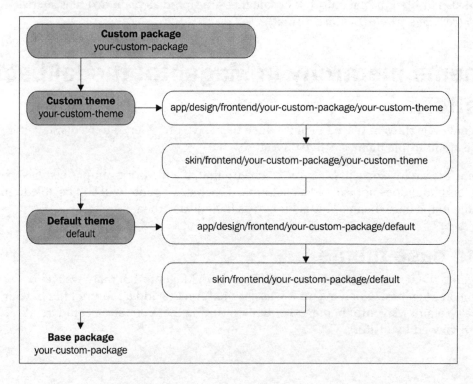

If the requested file is still not found by Magento, it reverts to the **base package**, looking in the `app/design/frontend/base/default` and `skin/frontend/base/default` directories. As a last resort, if the file is not found in any of these packages, Magento will respond with a rendering error, as it can't find a requested file needed to display itself.

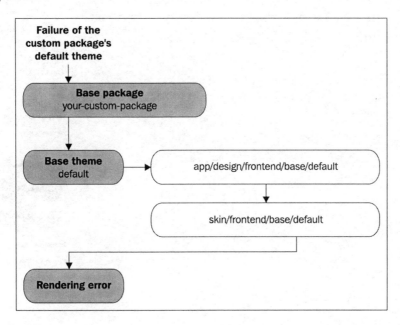

The Blank theme

The Blank theme is particularly useful to web designers creating custom Magento themes as it strips Magento back to its basics and allows you to see the basic components of a Magento store without the fuss of a more complex theme.

The Blank theme for Magento was originally available through Magento Connect but in Magento 1.4 it comes installed by default. You will find the Blank theme in the /app/design/frontend/default/blank and /skin/frontend/default/blank directory of your Magento installation.

 While many designers used the Blank theme as the base of their custom Magento theme for Magento 1.3 and below, it's advisable *not* to do this in Magento 1.4 as it will make your theme *less likely to be upgrade-proof* in the future.

Installing and activating a Magento theme

One of the fundamental tasks for a Magento theme designer is to be able to install and activate a theme. Firstly, chose a theme from the Magento Connect community at `http://www.magentocommerce.com/magento-connect/filter/community/design`. For this example, you'll be using the Blank theme available at `http://www.magentocommerce.com/magento-connect/Magento+Core/extension/518/blank-theme`:

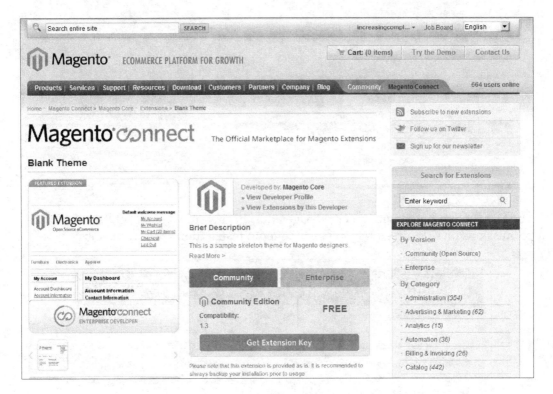

 The Blank theme is already installed in Magento 1.4, but provides an easy example to display package installation and activation within Magento.

If you select **Get Extension Key**, you will be provided with a text value that you can use in your Magento store's administration area to download the theme automatically through Magento Connect.

Installing a Magento theme

Once you have the Extension Key, log in to your Magento administration panel and navigate to **System | Magento Connect | Magento Connect Manager**:

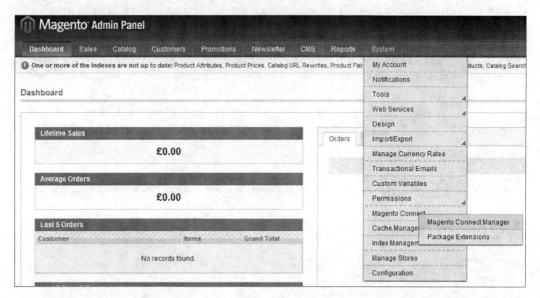

You may be presented with an error page after this if you have not set the correct file permissions on sub-directories in your Magento installation's root directory:

Once you've corrected this, if necessary, **Refresh** the page and you will be presented with the **Magento Connect Manager**:

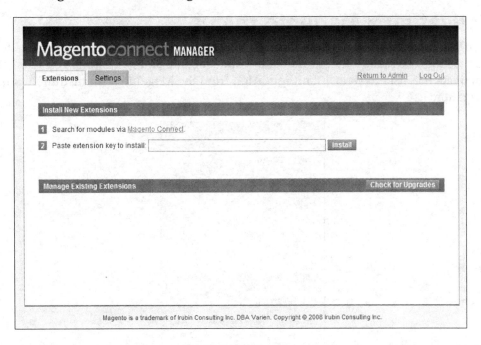

Under **Install New Extensions**, you need to paste the extension key for the package in to the **Paste extension key to install** field. Finally, click on the **Install** button and you will see the progress displayed beneath:

```
☑ Auto-scroll console contents
downloading Interface_Frontend_Default_Blank-1.4.1.0.tgz ...
Starting to download Interface_Frontend_Default_Blank-1.4.1.0.tgz (50,882 bytes)
. . . . . . . . . . . . ...done: 50,882 bytes
downloading Mage_Core_Modules-1.4.1.1.tgz ...
Starting to download Mage_Core_Modules-1.4.1.1.tgz (1,851,079 bytes)
...done: 1,851,079 bytes
```

Your theme is now installed; next step is to activate it.

Activating a Magento theme

Once you have installed a theme through Magento Connect, it will not be visible to your visitors. To make a theme visible to your Magento store's visitors, you will need to activate it. Select **System** | **Configuration** from the Magento administration panel navigation:

On the left, select the **Design** option from under **GENERAL**:

Here, you need to tell Magento which package to display. As you've seen before, you can assign a package at two levels: website level and store view level. Set this package at website level as the example store only contains store view for this example. The first step is to define the **Current Configuration Scope** in the top-left of the administration panel as **Main Website**. This defines your store's interface in your store:

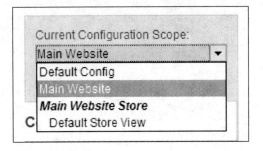

You now need to define values under the **Themes** section, which you may need to expand to see. It's worth noting that you need to leave the **Current Package Name** field as **default**. The remaining values—**Translations, Templates, Skin (Images/CSS), Layout,** and **Default** to **blank**:

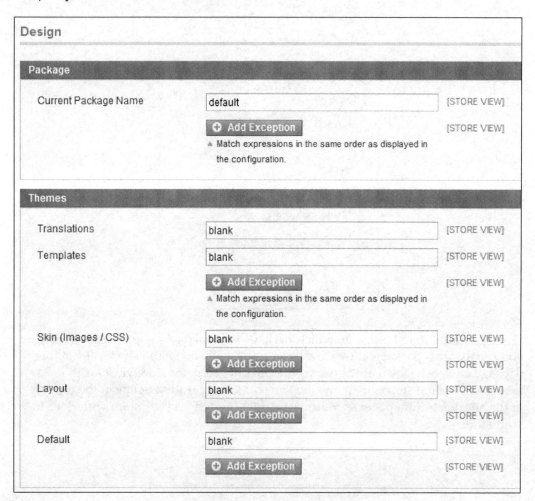

If you refresh the frontend of your Magento store now, you'll see the newly activated theme displayed:

Can't see your theme?
If you can't see your new theme once activated, you may need to disable Magento's cache, which is covered in the next chapter.

If you want to change these at the theme level of your Magento store, simply select the **Default Store View** or equivalent value nested under the relevant value in the **Current Configuration Scope** drop-down:

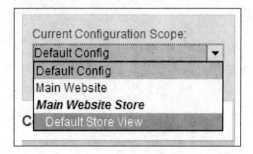

If you now navigate again to the **Design** tab, you will be able to configure the theme assigned at this level of your store in a similar manner to the interface level configuration you saw previously.

Good practice in Magento theming

There are a number of points that a good Magento theme will typically abide by:

- The use of only one layout file called `local.xml`, where any layout updates specific to the custom Magento theme are declared. Additionally, it is considered bad practice to create any layout files with the same name as any layout file in Magento's base theme.

- Similarly, there should be no CSS files within your theme's skin that use the same name as any CSS file in the default skin.

- Restricting any `.phtml` (Magento template files) to just those which have been changed for use with the custom theme.

Adhering to these guidelines of Magento theming make it easier to upgrade your Magento installation without making changes to your theme files.

Summary

You've now looked in to how a Magento theme works in theory, including the following:

- Terminology used in Magento themes
- The elements that make up a Magento theme
- What is the theme hierarchy in Magento, and how it works
- Some good practice guidelines to consider when creating a custom Magento theme
- What Magento's Blank theme is
- Installing and activating a Magento theme using Magento Connect

In the next chapters, you will begin customizing Magento themes and look in to Magento theming in more detail.

3
Magento Theme Basics

Now that you've looked at what Magento has to offer in terms of themes, how themes in Magento work, and the terminology you can use to describe the various aspects of Magento themes, you can begin to look at customizing the look and feel of your store. In this chapter, we'll cover the following:

- What Magento's cache does, and how to disable it to create a theme more easily
- Changing your store's logo
- Customizing your store's favicon
- Configuring the default product image
- Setting a watermark image for Magento to automatically apply to product images in your store

Magento's cache

As you've seen already, Magento is a large, powerful e-commerce system. While it offers a huge array of features, it can become slow to load for your customers: one way that Magento offers to mitigate this is a built-in caching system. Magento's cache reduces the number of files that need to be reloaded when a page in your store is requested.

Magento's caching system is fairly comprehensive and covers the following:

- Configuration files: refreshing this cache updates Magento's configuration files
- Theme files:
    ◦ Layout files: refreshing this cache updates any of the currently activated themes
    ◦ HTML output for blocks
    ◦ Locales (that is, translations)

- Collections
- Catalog:
    - ° Catalog rewrites: refreshing this cache regenerates search engine friendly URLs for products within Magento's catalog
    - ° Images: refreshing this cache regenerates automatically watermarked and resized images for products within Magento's catalog
    - ° Layered Navigation: refreshing this cache regenerates the index for layered navigation within your Magento store

The options that are relevant to us come under the theme files caching.

Disabling Magento's cache

While Magento's cache is useful when your store is 'live' and selling to customers, it can become inconvenient when you're developing your new Magento theme.

Log in to your Magento store's administration panel, and select **System** | **Cache Management**:

Magento's **Cache Storage Management** screen will then appear:

Next, you need to select the **Layouts**, **Blocks HTML Output**, and **Translations** options from the table:

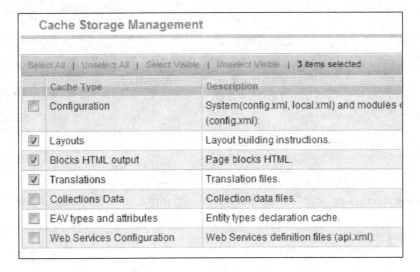

Each of the caches you selected controls a particular aspect of Magento's caching system that is related to theming:

- **Layouts**: This option controls the caching for your Magento themes' layout XML files, which tell Magento which blocks to add to your store's pages and where.

- **Blocks HTML output**: This option controls the caching for the Magento template files (.phtml) that make up both the overall skeleton HTML of your store (for example, the header, footer, and column areas), as well as the component blocks (for example, the search box, and the shopping cart).

- **Translations**: This option controls any changes you make to your store's locale files and in the core_translate *database table*, which control translations of your store's content.

To complete the disabling of these caches, select the value **Disable** from the **Actions** drop-down, and then click on the **Submit** button:

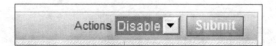

Once the Magento administration panel has refreshed itself, you should see that the **Layouts**, **Blocks HTML Output**, and **Translations** caches appear red rather than green and are marked as **DISABLED** under the **Status** column:

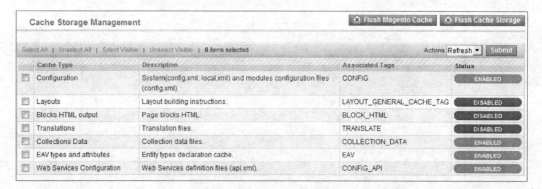

That's it, the necessary caches are disabled for theming your Magento store.

Re-enabling the caches

Once your Magento store is ready to launch, it's recommended that you re-enable these caches to minimize the load on your server.

Changing your store's logo

A common task in any theme work is changing the logo that is displayed on your store. By default, when using a fresh installation of Magento with the Default theme enabled, you will see the Magento logo in place of your own logo:

Log in to your Magento store's administration panel. If your Magento store is installed at `http://www.example.com/magento`, your administration panel is accessible from `http://www.example.com/magento/admin`. Once you have logged in successfully, choose **System | Configuration** from the navigation menu:

From here, select the **Design** option from under **GENERAL** in the left-hand column of the screen:

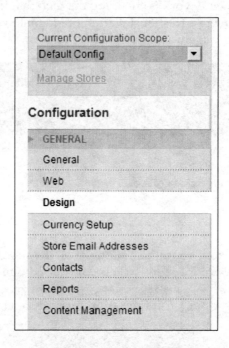

Next, select the **Header** option to the right to reveal three options:

- **Logo Image Src**
- **Logo Image Alt**
- **Welcome Text**

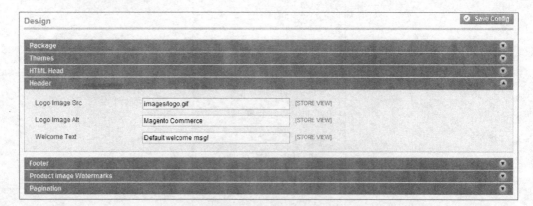

The first value, **Logo Image Src**, refers to the path of the store's logo, which is currently set to `images/logo.gif`. This path is relative to the following directory, assuming that the default interface enabled is known as `default: skin/frontend/ default/default`. Our new store's logo is for the M2 example store mentioned previously:

It's best practice to leave the default logo, `logo.gif`, as it is, so we'll upload our file in to the `skin/frontend/default/default/images` directory named as `m2-store-logo.gif`:

The second value here, **Logo Image Alt**, is what controls the content of the `alt` attribute for the logo's `img` element. Ideally, we therefore want to change this value to the name of our store:

Finally, the **Welcome Text** field allows you to customize what appears to customers on your store who are not logged in. In Magento's Default theme, this is displayed above the user account links, to the right-hand side in your store's header:

We'll change this to **Welcome to the M2 Store**:

Finally, you can click on the **Save Config** button, located in the top-right of your screen to save these changes:

If you now refresh the frontend of your store, you'll see the new logo appear at the top-left of the store's design:

You will also be able to see the changed **Welcome Text** message at the top-right of your screen:

That's it, you've successfully changed your Magento store's logo!

Changing your store's logo using a static block in Magento

It is also possible to use a static block within Magento's content management feature to control your store's logo, see the guide on the Magento Commerce wiki at: `http://www.magentocommerce.com/wiki/4_-_themes_and_template_customization/page_templates/how_to_change_the_logo_and_header_image_to_a_static_block`.

Note that this technique is not recommended if you are likely to use your Magento theme across various installations, as it's not quite as portable as changing the settings in **System | Configuration | Design** as you did before, as you would need to create the static block in each installation and add your logo's image file to it.

Changing your store's favicon

Alongside changing your store's logo, changing its favicon is a relatively simple step you can take to customizing your Magento store and differentiating it from both your competitors and others using the Magento platform.

What is a favicon?

A **favicon** is a 'favorites icon', a graphic measuring 16 x 16 pixels in dimension which is usually displayed in your browser's address bar, next to the URL of the current page you are looking at:

Favicons are particularly useful for differentiating your store's website from other websites in customer's bookmark lists. Effective favicons are generally as follows:

- Eye-catching: Your favicon might be seen in a huge selection of tabs a customer has opened in their browser or a large list of bookmarked websites

- Simple: 16 x 16 pixels is a very small space to design in and crowded designs don't work well! In particular, scaling down your store's logo to the correct size rarely works well as a favicon; rather, creating a custom graphic which is either a part of your store's logo or using an abstract element of your store's design such as a block of colors or an initial of your store's name will work better than an illegible, pixilated version of your logo.

- Consistent with the design of your website: A consistent favicon can help to reinforce the trustworthiness of your store by presenting a reliable, stable view of your business to customers. In general, the more consistent the look and feel of every element of your store is, the safer a customer is likely to feel when ordering from your store.

It can be worth experimenting with different variations of favicons for your Magento store before settling on the preferred design.

Favicon inspiration

There are a number of websites dedicated to favicon designs that you can turn to for inspiration. Firstly, there is The Favicon Gallery (`http://thefavicongallery.com`), which displays favicons in a grid. This is useful in determining which techniques make a favicon design stand out from others:

The **Favicon** Gallery

454 Favicons registered - Submit a Favicon*   What is a Favicon ?

page 1 2   vivabit.co.uk

click on the favicon to select it

Secondly, there is Fineicons' Favicon Gallery (`http://www.fineicons.com/en/favicon-gallery`). This website categorizes favicons in to three columns; displaying them by appearance (**Symbol**, **Typographical**, or **Other**):

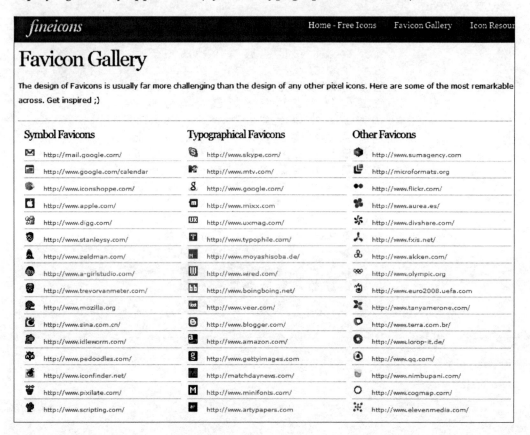

Changing the favicon

Now that you have an overview of what a favicon is and why they can be useful for your store, let's go about changing your store's favicon. By default, the Magento logo is used as your store's favicon (next to the `http://demo.magentocommerce.com/` text):

If you look in the `<head>` element of your Magento store's HTML source, you'll see the following two lines of HTML, assuming Magento is installed at `http://www.example.com/magento/`:

```
<link rel="icon" href="http:// www.example.com /magento/skin/frontend/
default/default/favicon.ico" type="image/x-icon" />
<link rel="shortcut icon" href="http://www.example.com/magento/skin/
frontend/default/default/favicon.ico" type="image/x-icon" />
```

This means that you can replace the file called `favicon.ico` in the `skin/frontend/default/default/` directory with our new favicon file:

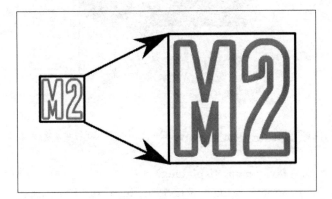

Favicon files need to be in the `.ico` format; one option for converting your file to this format for use with your Magento store is an online favicon generator such as Dynamic Drive's Favicon Generator, available at `http://tools.dynamicdrive.com/favicon/`.

Other favicon formats

It is possible to use other file formats such as PNG and GIF for your store's favicon, but the ICO (`.ico`) format is more likely to work, especially in older versions of Internet Explorer.

Once you have uploaded the new favicon file, refresh your store and you should see your new favicon displayed:

That's it, your store's new favicon is ready!

New favicon not displaying?

If you don't see the new favicon file in your browser, try viewing the file directly in your browser (for example, visit `http://www.example.com/magento/skin/frontend/default/default/favicon.ico`) and refreshing it.

Displaying products on the homepage

Before we get in to greater detail in theming your Magento store, it will be useful to add products to your store's homepage. By default, your Magento installation will not display products on your website's homepage, but static content that is populated through Magentos' Content Management System (CMS). We want our store's customers to see a selection of featured products from our store. To do this, you will have to go through the following steps:

1. Adding a root category called 'Featured'.

2. Adding one or more products to this category.

3. Updating your store's layout to reflect this on the homepage.

[76]

Adding the featured category

Log in to your store's administration panel and navigate to **Catalog | Manage Categories**:

Look to the left-hand side of the subsequent screen and select **Add Root Category** under the **Categories** heading:

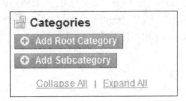

You will now see the **New Category** screen appear:

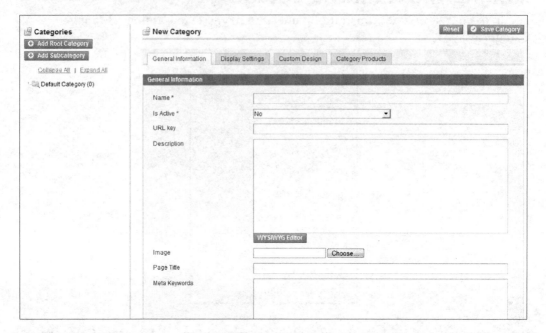

Here, you will need to complete the very basics of the form in the **General Information** section. Firstly, enter the name of the category (**Featured**) in the **Name** field and change the **Is Active** field to **Yes**. Next, add a description to the **Description** field if you wish to (this field is optional), and optionally select an **Image** for the category itself:

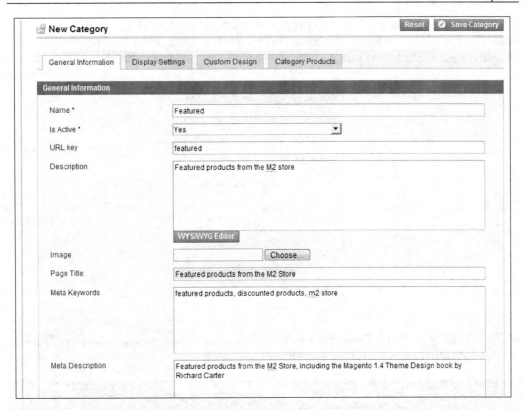

Finally, change the value of the **Include in Navigation Menu** to **No** and click on the **Save Category** button at the top-left of the screen to ensure your category is created:

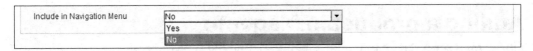

The next step in adding a featured products category to your Magento store's homepage is to ensure there are products in your featured category. Remaining in Magento's administration panel, navigate to **Catalog | Manage Products**:

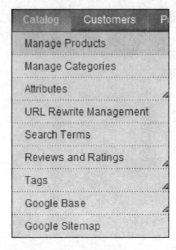

In the resulting **Manage Products** screen that loads, create a new product by clicking the **Add Product** button at the top-right of the screen:

Adding a product in Magento

Next, you'll see a screen that allows you to define the type of product you're adding. At this point, it is assumed your store uses the simple product type, but this will work with other product types too:

- Grouped Product
- Configurable Product
- Virtual Product
- Bundle Product
- Downloadable Product

As such, all you need to do at this stage is to click on the **Continue** button towards the bottom of the screen:

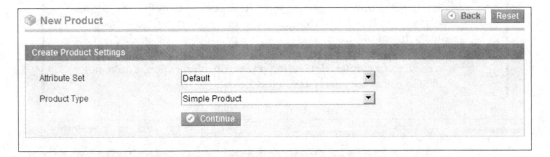

You now need to complete the **New Product (Default)** form. Make sure that you enter values for the required fields, which are as follows:

- **Name**, the name of your product as it will appear to customers.

- **Description**, a detailed description for your product, that is typically displayed in the product view page for customers to read.

- **Short Description**, that is typically used as a summary of products on pages where multiple products are displayed.

- **SKU** (Stock Keeping Unit), that is useful to maintain a reference to your product for your own systems.

- **Weight**, the weight of your product that is typically used in shipping cost calculations.

- **Status**, which needs to be set to **Enabled** in order for your product to be displayed in your store.

- **Visibility**, which controls whether Magento displays the product in search results for your store's search feature and whether it appears in Magento's catalog pages too. Usually, it's recommended that you keep the value **Catalog, Search** for this field.

URL key field

It's also recommended using the **URL key** field to define the address of your product within Magento. For example, if you give this field the value of `m2-test-product`, the product would be displayed at `http://www.example.com/magento/a-category/m2-test-product` or similar, depending on your configuration. You're not able to use space characters in this field.

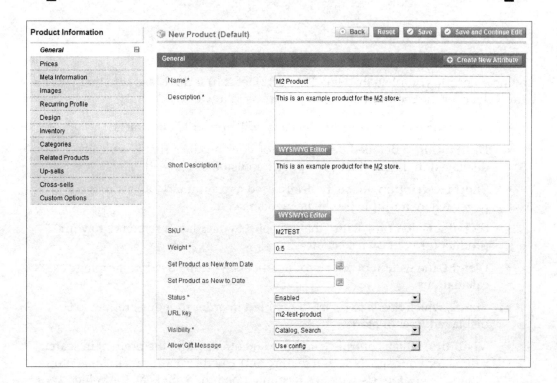

The next step is to define the prices you want to set for your product. Look in the column to the left of the screen, and select **Prices** from the list:

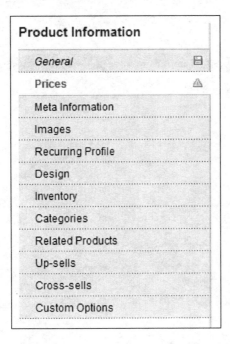

Within the **Prices** section, you will find that there are two required fields:

- **Price**, which allows you to define the cost of the product to the customer. Note that the currency code, as configured when you installed Magento, is displayed beneath the field (it is shown as **GBP**, Great British Pounds in the following screenshot).

- **Tax Class**, which allows you to configure tax options for the product, if necessary. For this example, assume the product has a tax class of **None**.

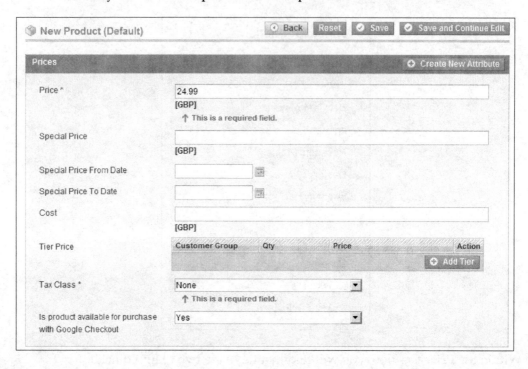

Finally, navigate to the **Categories** tab (to the left-hand side of the screen) within this product:

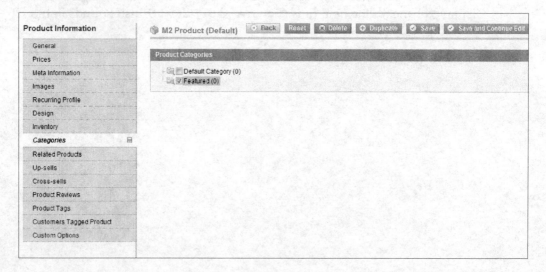

To finish creating the new product, click on the **Save** button to the top-right of the screen. That's it, your product is now in your Magento store and in the **Featured** category!

Finding your category's ID

You will need the ID number of the featured category you created earlier for the next step of this task. To find the category's ID, navigate to **Catalog | Manage Categories** and select the **Featured** category from the list of categories on the left-hand side of the screen:

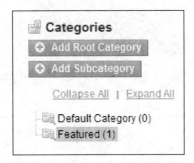

Once the next screen loads, the ID is displayed next to the name of the category in the header of the page:

So in the example store, the ID for the featured category is **3**.

Adding the featured category to the homepage

Now you need to add the featured product category to your store's homepage. To do this, navigate to **CMS** | **Pages** in your store's administration panel:

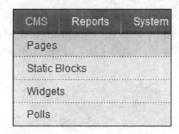

Under the **Title** column of pages listed, select the **Home page** from the list to edit its contents:

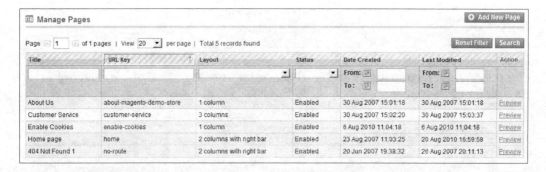

By default, the page will show the **Page Information** tab. Select the **Content** option from the left of the screen:

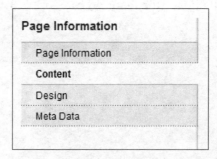

Once this has loaded, you will need to add the following code in to the content area:

```
{{block type="catalog/product_list" template="catalog/product/list.
phtml" category_id="3" }}
```

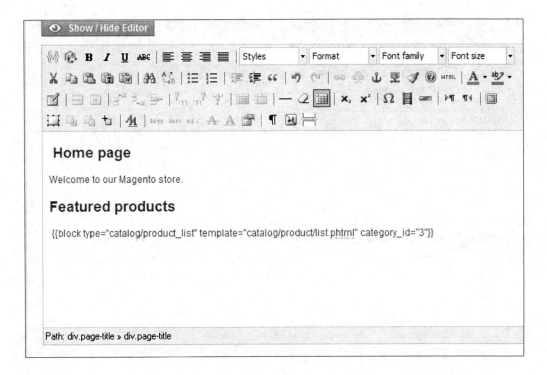

You may find that you need to hide Magento's Rich Text Editor (RTE), which you can do by clicking the **Show / Hide Editor** button to the top-left of the content field:

You will then see the text-only editor, which presents a mixture of raw HTML and Magento 'markup':

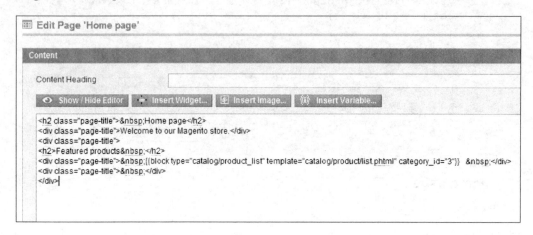

If you now click on the **Save** button and visit the frontend of your Magento store and refresh the page, you will see the products from the category you defined before, displayed in the page:

If you have not added any products to the featured products category you created earlier, you will see that Magento displays an error message:

That's it, you now have a featured products category displayed on your Magento store's homepage.

Customizing the default placeholder product image

Take for example, the product we added before to test our featured products category for the store's homepage:

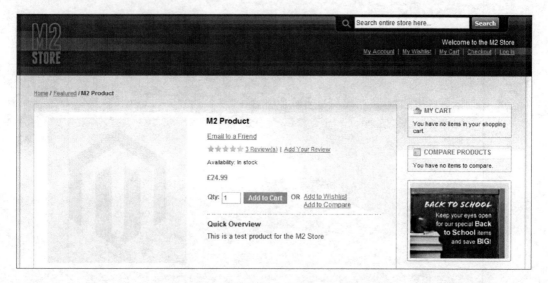

If you do not specify a photograph for a product in Magento when creating it, Magento uses a generic image in its place. By default, the image is a watermarked Magento logo:

Magento uses three sizes of these images across your store: the large size, a smaller size, and a thumbnail size. The image files are stored in the `skin/frontend/base/default/images/catalog/product/placeholder/` directory of your Magento installation.

Theme hierarchy refresher

If you need a refresher on theme hierarchy in Magento, look back at *Chapter 2, Exploring Magento Themes*.

As always, it's better to avoid making changes to the base theme to make your theme update-proof, so copy these files in to your custom theme's directory. For example, if you're modifying Magento's Default theme, you will need to copy these images to the `skin/frontend/default/default/images/catalog/product/placeholder/` directory of your Magento installation.

Default theme

Magento's Default theme already contains these images in the relevant directory, so you can start modifying or overwriting them at will.

You will now need to overwrite or customize the product images. By default, the sizes for these images are as follows:

- 262 x 262 pixels for the large size image (`image.jpg`)
- 135 x 135 pixels for the small size image (`small_image.jpg`)
- 50 x 50 pixels for the thumbnail image (`thumbnail.jpg`)

It's a good idea to make use of your store's logo in the default product image to help maintain a consistency in the look and feel of your store for customers, as this can help to create a more trustworthy look to your business and increase consumer confidence:

If you now refresh the product page once you have uploaded the new images to your store, you'll see the new placeholder image appear:

Customizing the product image watermark

Apart from allowing customization of the default product image in your store, Magento also permits the addition of a custom watermark image that can be applied over the top of the product photographs in your store. By default, Magento does not apply a watermark image to product photographs in your store. To add a custom watermark image to your store, navigate to **System** | **Configuration** in your Magento store's administration panel:

Next, locate the **Design** option from the panel on the left-hand side of your screen:

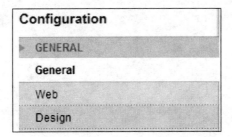

Now select the **Product Image Watermarks** from the primary content area, so that the fields for that section appear as follows:

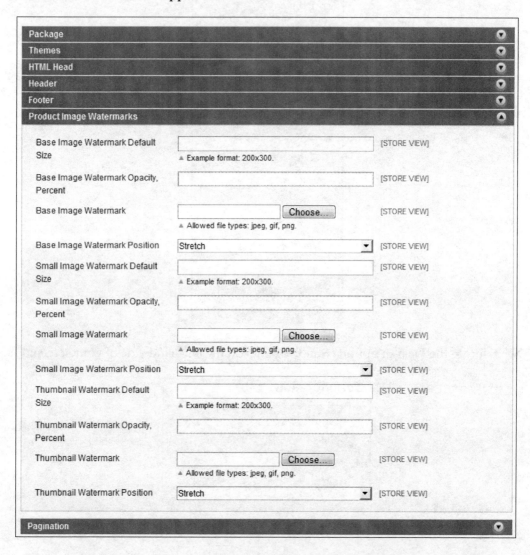

There are four types of field here. Firstly, there are fields which allow you to define the size of the watermark being applied (for example, **Base Image Watermark Default Size**). Secondly, there are opacity fields (for example, **Base Image Watermark Opacity, Percent**), that allow you to define the opacity (that is, how strongly the watermark image appears over the product photograph). Thirdly, the watermark field (for example, **Base Image Watermark**) that allows you to upload an image from your computer to use as the watermark image.

The last field type used here is position (for example, **Base Image Watermark Position**), which allows you to customize where and how the watermark image is positioned in relation to the photograph of the product (the values provided are **Stretch, Tile, Top/Left, Top/Right, Bottom/Left, Bottom/Right, Center**).

For the purposes of this example, only the larger (**Base**) image will have a watermark image applied, which is based on the default product image created previously:

Specify the image you wish to use as the watermark and a low number for the opacity (**25** is a fairly good higher boundary with most images). In this instance, we'll use the **Tile** option for the **Position** field so that the watermark repeats over our image:

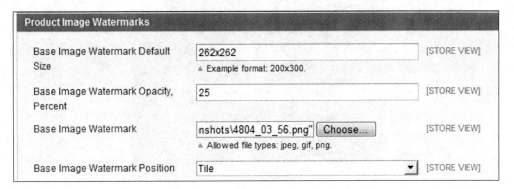

If you now refresh a page in your store, the watermark should appear on larger images when they are displayed (such as on the product view):

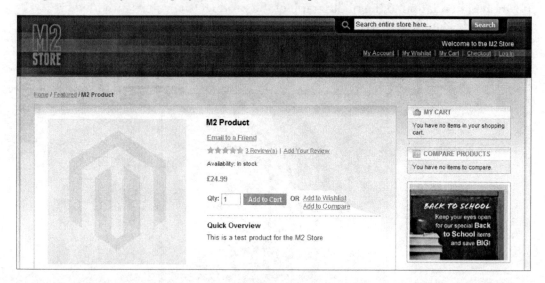

You may find it hard to see the watermark. If the preceding screenshot is enlarged by 400%, you can see a faint **M2** logo over the default product image:

If the watermark does not appear, navigate to **System | Cache Management** in your Magento administration panel and click on **Flush Catalog Images Cache** under the **Additional Cache Management** options:

Additional Cache Management

Flush Catalog Images Cache Pregenerated product images files.

Flush JavaScript/CSS Cache Themes JavaScript and CSS files combined to one file.

Summary

In this chapter, you began to look in to customizing your Magento store with content including:

- An overview of Magento's cache, and a guide on how to disable it
- How to change your store's logo
- Customizing a Magento store's favicon (favorites icon)
- Configuring the default product image in your store
- How to set a watermark image to overlay product images within your store

In coming chapters, you'll again look at customizing Magento themes to suit your needs.

4

Magento Theme Layouts

You've seen some reasonably simple techniques to customize your Magento store, so now is the time to delve deeper into Magento theming. This chapter covers the following:

- Definitions for layout terminology in Magento
- Enabling template path hints to help you customize more easily
- Enabling block name hints
- An introduction to XML
- Changing page layout in Magento through XML layout

This chapter will focus on customizing an existing Magento theme more, subsequent chapters cover beginning a Magento theme from scratch.

Magento layout terminology

Layout files in Magento define which content blocks, as defined in Magento template files (`.phtml`), are positioned within Magento skeleton templates (which are also in the `.phtml` format), that define the overall structure of your store's theme. Magento layout files are in the XML format (`.xml`) and are located in the `app/design/frontend/your_interface/your_theme/layout/` directory of your Magento installation.

While you will encounter more definitions used to differentiate between aspects of layout within Magento, there are two definitions of use at this point:

1. Default layout
2. Layout updates

Default layout

Default layout in Magento refers to the pre-existing layout that defines the blocks throughout your Magento theme: default layout tells your store exactly in which structural block (for example, header, footer, left-column) to place the smaller blocks (for example, search box, **My Cart** block, newsletter subscription form, page content) and is generally defined in your Magento installation's base theme.

Layout updates

Layout updates in Magento overwrite the default layout for specific views in Magento, such as the checkout page or the product details view. In Magento, layout updates are used to change the base theme's layout part by part instead of entirely overwriting the layout defined. For instance, your theme may use a layout update to change the blocks displayed in a column in your theme for a specific page such as your store's homepage, but for other pages Magento's default layout will be used to determine which blocks appear where in your page.

Template Path Hints and Block Name Hints

As you've seen, Magento themes can be baffling to those who are unfamiliar with how Magento and Magento themes work. Useful tools to help overcome this when developing Magento themes are **Template Path Hints** and **Block Name Hints**. The Template Path Hints displays the (relative) path to each of your store's blocks within Magento's theme directory structure, that makes it easier for you as a Magento theme designer to customize the necessary files to change your Magento theme.

Enabling Template Path Hints

Enabling **Template Path Hints** displays the path to each template used within your Magento theme. To enable this feature of Magento, log in to your Magento store's administration panel and navigate to **System | Configuration**:

Next, you will need to change the **Current Configuration Scope** to **Main Website** or **Default Store View** as the option is unavailable in the **Default Config** scope:

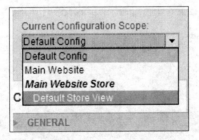

From the left-hand column, select **Developer** from under the **ADVANCED** options:

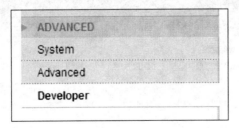

If you now enlarge the **Debug** section in the right-hand column of the page, you should see three options as follows:

- **Profiler**
- **Template Path Hints**
- **Add Block Names to Hints**

At the moment, you only need to use the **Template Path Hints** option, so uncheck the checkbox next to it and select **Yes** from the drop-down field to enable this feature:

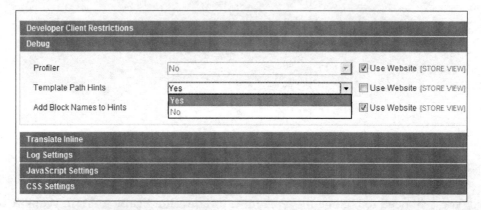

If you now click the **Save Config** button at the top-right of your screen, **Template Path Hints** should be enabled. To see them, simply refresh your Magento store's frontend:

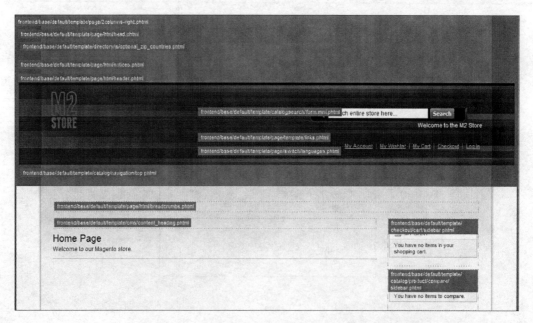

You'll also see that the footer has the relevant file paths displayed:

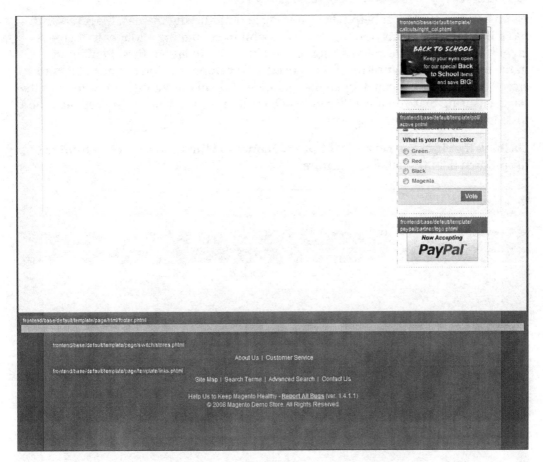

That's it, Magento **Template Path Hints** are enabled now. If you look at the search form, you'll see that the template path displayed relates to the path relative to the root of your Magento installation, the value is: **frontend/base/default/template/ catalogsearch/form.mini.phtml**:

Other templates are displayed similarly, allowing you to see exactly where specific blocks in your Magento theme are held, which can greatly help when developing simple Magento themes.

Enabling Block Name Hints

As an additional layer of help when creating and modifying themes, Magento also has a **Block Name Hints** option, which is useful in debugging a Magento theme's layout, as it displays the `name` attribute used in Magento layout files. Remaining in the **System** | **Configuration** | **Advanced** | **Developer** section of your Magento store's administration panel, open the **Debug** section in the right-hand column of the page, ensuring that you are either in the **Default Store View** or **Main Website** scope instead of the **Default Config** scope.

Uncheck the checkbox next to **Add Block Names to Hints** and select **Yes** from the drop-down field to enable this feature.

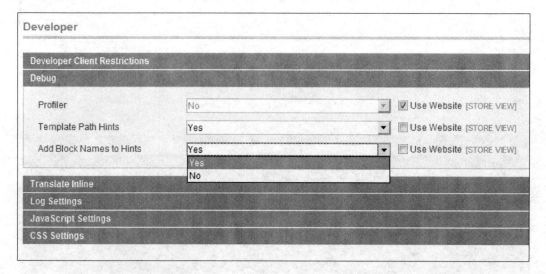

Save this change by clicking **Save Config** at the top-right of your screen (you can leave **Template Path Hints** set to **Yes**). If you now look at the frontend of your Magento store, you'll see that the block name hints have appeared, displayed to the top-right of each block:

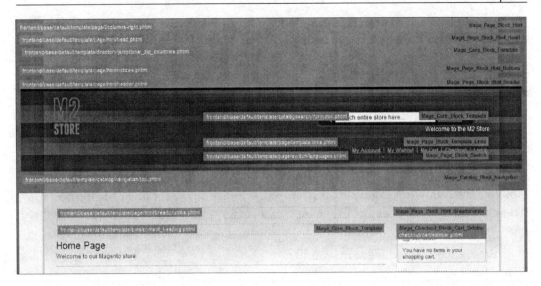

The footer area also has the block and template path name values displayed in a similar manner:

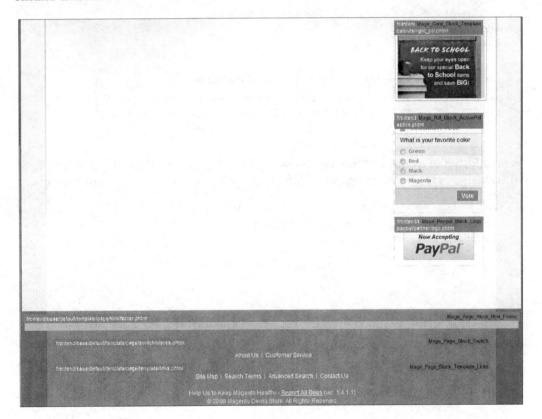

If you again look at the search feature, now with **Block Name Hints** enabled, you see that the value for the block name is displayed as **Mage_Core_Block_Template**:

```
frontend/base/default/template/catalogsearch/form.mini.phtml ch entire store here...        Mage_Core_Block_Template
```

The block name hints show you how the block is classed within the framework used to build Magento. So, `Mage_Core_Block_Template` tells you that this block is classed as a 'block template' within Magento, which is useful when it comes to defining the `type` attribute in your theme's layout files. Corresponding layout for this block may look like the following example taken from the `catalogsearch.xml` file in the `/app/design/frontend/base/default/layout` directory, with the `type` attribute defined as `core/template`:

```
<reference name="header">
 <block
  type="core/template"
  name=»top.search»
  as="topSearch"
  template="catalogsearch/form.mini.phtml"/>
</reference>
```

> **More information on block names**
> You can find more information on block names and others in the Magento documentation at `http://docs.magentocommerce.com`.

As an additional example, take the following XML layout file, that adds a static block called `widget` created in Magento's CMS at the right-hand column of your theme:

```
<reference name="right">
 <block type="cms/block" name="widget" after="-">
  <action method="setBlockId">
   <block_id>widget</block_id>
  </action>
  </block>
</reference>
```

Here the **type** attribute tells Magento to expect `cms/block` type content, that is displayed in the block name hints tools as `Mage_Cms_Block_Widget_Block`.

In contrast to the template path hints, which displayed the relative path within your Magento installation, the block name hints display a more abstract value which is used in Magento XML layout files.

Restricting who can see the hints

The template path hints and block name hints are really useful for theme designers such as yourself, but they could cause confusion if you're working on a live Magento store to make minor changes. Luckily, Magento allows you to specify IP addresses that are able to see these hints, leaving usual customers to browse your store uninterrupted.

Within the **System | Configuration** area of Magento's administration panel, remain in the **Advanced | Developer** area you were previously viewing to enable template path hints and block name hints. Expand the **Developer Client Restrictions** section of the page:

Uncheck the checkbox for the **Use Website** field, and enter your IP address(es) in to the **Allowed IPs (comma separated)** field:

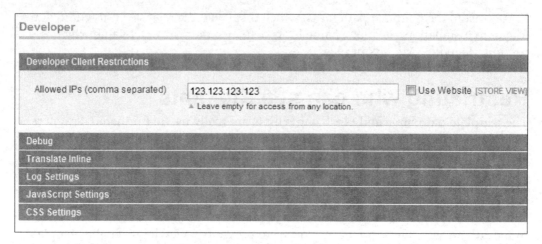

If you want to allow multiple IP addresses to view this feature of Magento, simply separate them with a comma, such as `123.123.123.123, 123.123.123.124`.

Finding your own IP

You can detect your IP by using a service such as **What Is My IP?** (`http://www.whatismyip.com`) or **What Is My IP Address?** (`http://whatismyipaddress.com`).

You should now be able to see the block name hints and template path hints, while others looking at your Magento store will not see these.

A brief guide to XML

Layout files in Magento make use of XML—eXtensible Markup Language. It can be baffling to see XML for the first time—especially if you're not familiar with XHTML, but it's quite simple.

There is one simple rule to creating well-formed XML: every element must close. An element in XML can close in two ways.

- The element can *self-close*
- The element can be *closed with a closing tag of its own type*

Self-closing elements in XML

A self-closing element in XML is an element which closes itself. Take as an example, the XML element `<thing>`. Normally, this element would look like the following:

```
<thing>Some optional data</thing>
```

If this element self-closed, it would look like the following:

```
<thing />
```

If you want to encapsulate data in the `<thing>` element, it might look like the following:

```
<thing data= "some data " />
```

Closing XML elements normally

The other way to close an XML element is with a closing tag of the opening tag's type. So, with the `<thing>` tag, a valid XML element would look like:

```
<thing>Value (if any)</thing>
```

Entity escapes in XML

As in HTML (Hyper Text Markup Language) and XHTML, XML requires some characters to be escaped to prevent data in the XML file from being misinterpreted. The characters that you'll need to watch out for in your XML file are:

Character	Description	Escape
&	Ampersand	&
<	Less than	<
>	Greater than	>
'	Apostrophe	'
"	Quotation mark	"

For example, if you wanted to display **A & B > C < D 'E' "F"** in our XML file, it would look like the following:

```
A &amp; B &gt; C &lt; D &apos;E&apos; &quot;F&quot;
```

Now that we have a better grasp of XML, we can look more closely at changing the layout using Magento's XML layout.

Changing a page's layout

There are three ways you can change the layout of a page within Magento:

1. On a page-per-page basis, if it is controlled through Magento's content management system (CMS), through a drop-down list of selectable page layouts

2. Through Magento's CMS, in the **Design** tab's **Layout Update XML** field

3. Through Magento's XML layout files

For your reference, both of these methods are covered next.

Changing a page's layout through Magento's administration panel

Log in to your Magento installation's administration panel (located at http://www.example.com/magento/admin if your installation of Magento is located at http://www.example.com/magento). Navigate to **CMS | Pages**:

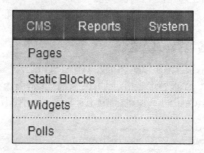

Here, you'll see a list of pages that are managed by Magento's CMS:

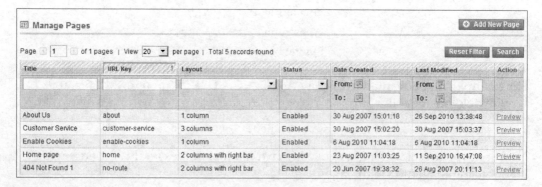

Title	URL Key	Layout	Status	Date Created	Last Modified	Action
				From: To:	From: To:	
About Us	about	1 column	Enabled	30 Aug 2007 15:01:18	26 Sep 2010 13:38:48	Preview
Customer Service	customer-service	3 columns	Enabled	30 Aug 2007 15:02:20	30 Aug 2007 15:03:37	Preview
Enable Cookies	enable-cookies	1 column	Enabled	6 Aug 2010 11:04:18	6 Aug 2010 11:04:18	Preview
Home page	home	2 columns with right bar	Enabled	23 Aug 2007 11:03:25	11 Sep 2010 16:47:08	Preview
404 Not Found 1	no-route	2 columns with right bar	Enabled	20 Jun 2007 19:38:32	26 Aug 2007 20:11:13	Preview

Take a note of the value **URL Key** that corresponds to the page with a value in the **Title** column of **About Us.** In this case, the value we need is **about**:

| About Us | about | 1 column | Enabled | 30 Aug 2007 15:01:18 | 26 Sep 2010 13:38:48 | Preview |

By default: imported sample data

This value is set to `about-magento-demo-store` if you've imported Magento's sample data in to your store.

To view this page in the frontend of your store (that is, the view that your customers will see), type the address of your Magento installation in to your browser's address bar and then append the value displayed in the **URL Key** column you just saw:

http://www.example.com/magento/about

Once the page is loaded, you will see that the **About Us** page has a three-column layout:

If you look more closely in Magento's administration panel, under the **Design** tab at the left-hand side (displayed once you are editing the page in Magento's CMS), however, you'll see that this page's layout is set to **1 column**:

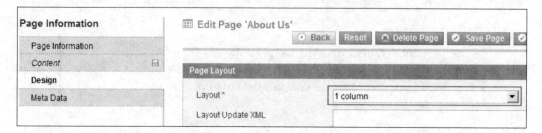

If you disable the editor with the **Show/Hide Editor** button and look at the HTML view in the text editor provided, you will see that the three columns are created within the content in the CMS, referencing CSS classes `.col3-set` that surrounds three `<div>`s; `.col-1`, `.col-2`, and `.col-3`:

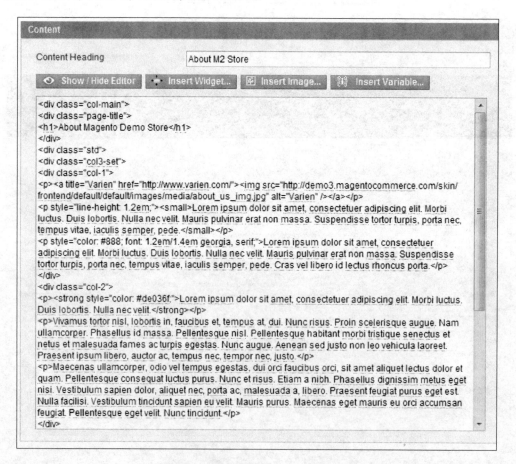

Switch back to the editor by clicking the **Show/Hide Editor** button again, replace the filler content for the about page with something relevant to your store:

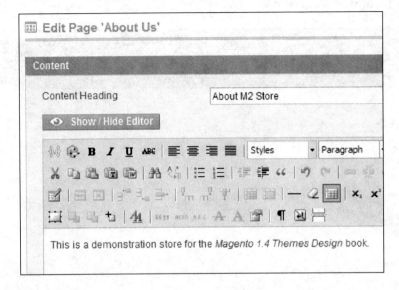

To change the page's layout, select the **Layout** drop-down list and select the **2 columns with left bar** option:

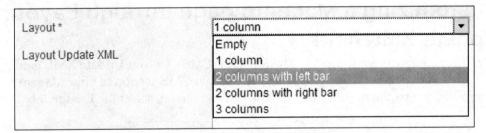

Click on the **Save Page** button to the top-right of the screen to complete the change:

If you now refresh the page on the frontend of your Magento store, you'll see the left column, containing a callout (advertisement) and a registration form for the newsletter feature of Magento:

Customizing a Magento page through Layout Update XML field

To change a page's layout through the Magento CMS's **Layout Update XML** field, navigate to the page you wish to change within the **CMS** section of your Magento administration panel. In the left-hand side of your screen, select the **Design** tab:

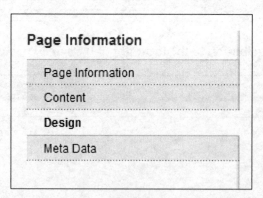

Prepare the XML layout you wish to use to change this specific page. In this case, you will add the 'callout' advertisement back to the left-hand column of your store:

```
<reference name="left">
 <block type="core/template" name="left.permanent.callout"
template="callouts/left_col.phtml" />
</reference>
```

If you now click on the **Save Page** button at the top-right of your administration panel and return to your Magento store's frontend to view the page you have just edited (in this example, it was the **About Us** page), you should see the callout appear in the page's left-hand column:

You successfully used the **Layout Update XML** field in Magento's CMS to change your store's layout!

Customizing a Magento page through layout files

While some pages in your Magento store can have their layout altered through the CMS, other pages must have their layout modified through Magento XML files. In this example, you will see how to change the layout of the checkout page in Magento. Firstly, look at the frontend of your store's **Checkout**:

> **Locating Magento's checkout**
>
> You can locate the checkout in your Magento store by clicking the link labeled **Checkout** below the search box in Magento's Default theme, or by visiting `http://www.example.com/magento/checkout/cart`, assuming your Magento installation is at `http://www.example.com/magento/`.

If you wanted to change the layout of this view in your Magento store to display two columns, we need to locate the layout file that controls this particular view. To do this, you may find it helpful to (re)enable the template path hints tool as described previously.

As the Default theme is currently in use on the store, the default layout for the checkout view is defined in the `checkout.xml` file in the `app/design/frontend/base/default/layout` directory. If you open this file, you'll see that the layout is defined within the `shopping_cart_index` handle with the following XML:

```
<reference name="root">
 <action method="setTemplate"><template>page/1column.phtml</
template></action>
</reference>
```

While in Magento 1.3 you might have edited the layout in this file directly, to make sure our version of Magento 1.4 is as upgrade-proof as possible, you will need to create a `checkout.xml` file in the Default package's directory: `app/design/frontend/default/default/layout`. You may find that you need to create the `/layout` sub-directory here, if no other layout changes have been made in this theme. In the new `checkout.xml` file, copy and paste the entirety of the old `checkout.xml` in the `app/design/frontend/base/default/layout` directory and locate the following XML:

```
<action method="setTemplate">
<template>page/1column.phtml</template>
</action>
```

Replace the value in the `<template>` element by changing this to the following:

```
<action method="setTemplate">
<template>page/2columns-left.phtml</template>
</action>
```

The path set within the `<template>` element is relative to the `/template` directory, following Magento's hierarchy you saw described in an earlier chapter. If you now refresh the checkout page once uploading the `checkout.xml` to the `app/design/frontend/default/default/layout` in your Magento installation, you should see the updated layout affect it:

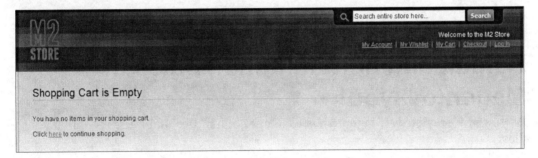

Notice that the left-hand column is empty: you will need to remove another line from the new `checkout.xml` file to see content appear here. Locate the lines that read:

```
<checkout_cart_index translate="label">
 <label>Shopping Cart</label>
 <remove name="right"/>
 <remove name="left"/>
```

Comment out the line that reads `<remove name="left"/>` as follows:

```
<checkout_cart_index translate="label">
<label>Shopping Cart</label>
<remove name="right"/>
<!--<remove name="left"/>-->
```

If you now upload this file again and refresh the **Checkout** page, you'll see the fully updated layout changes:

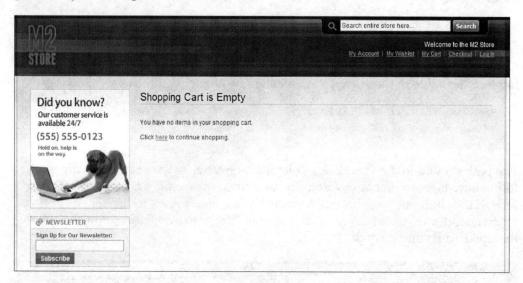

Default and non-default handles in Magento layout

As you saw previously, Magento has two types of **handles** that it uses within layout files:

1. **Default handles**, which affect (almost) every page in your Magento store
2. **Non-default handles**, which can be used to affect the layout of specific pages within your Magento store

What is a handle?

A handle is a reference name that Magento uses to refer to a particular view (or cluster of views) in your Magento store. For example, the `<cms_page>` handle used later controls the layout of pages in your Magento store created through the content management system (CMS).

The default handle

The `<default>` handle defines what is the default behavior for a layout within a particular view. So, if layout for the **Checkout** view in Magento is defined for the default handle to show a left-hand column in a two column layout, this is the layout that you will see in your store, unless you use a non-default handle to change the layout for a particular view in that Magento feature. For example, you could change the one-page **Checkout**'s view with a non-default handle to help simplify a customer's options when it comes to checking out from your store.

Non-default handles

If the handle is not `<default>`, the updates in the nested XML beneath it will apply to the relevant page(s) in your Magento store. Let's have a look at part of the `cms.xml` XML layout file from Magento, located in the `app/design/frontend/base/default/layout` directory:

```
<layout version="0.1.0">
<!-- omitted layout XML -->

    <cms_page>
        <!-- omitted layout XML -->
        <reference name="content">
            <block type="cms/page" name="cms_page"/>
        </reference>
<!-- omitted layout XML -->
    </cms_page>
<!-- omitted layout XML -->
</layout>
```

> **Layout handles for CMS pages**
>
> Magento does not provide a layout handle for each page in your Magento store, so it's actually only possible to affect all CMS-controlled pages in your store through XML layout file changes, though you can change individual page's layout through the CMS interface as described previously.

The `<default>` handle applies layout to any page which has its layout defined by the `cms.xml` file. The non-default handle in the layout is `<cms_page>`, which controls the layout for pages created in Magento's CMS. The previous layout simply tells Magento where to insert the page's content.

Useful handles in Magento

Some useful layout handles in Magento—the identifiers which allow you to single out a particular page or section of your Magento store are as follows:

XML handle	Page it identifies in Magento	XML layout file the XML handle is referenced in
catalog_category_default	The default view for a category of products.	catalog.xml
customer_account	The customer account page, shown when a customer is logged in to their account on your store.	customer.xml
catalog_product_view	The product page view (that is, a page which displays an individual product).	catalog.xml
cms_page	Pages created with Magento's content management system.	cms.xml
checkout_cart_index	The checkout's 'index' (that is, default) view	checkout.xml
cms_index_defaultnoroute	The default error page for the 404 'not found' error	cms.xml
cms_index_defaultindex	The homepage of your Magento store	cms.xml

There are many other handles available to you, but as Magento expands these will change and evolve.

As you're only wanting to theme Magento, you shouldn't have to change these handles (instead, you will be referencing them in layout files), but it can still be useful to know what they do.

Summary

In this chapter, you've looked into what template path hints and block name hints can do to help us theme Magento and in to the basics of a Magento theme's layout files:

- Some useful definitions used in Magento for layout
- Customizing layout using the CMS and by editing Magento XML layout files
- A guide to handles within Magento layout files
- An introduction to XML
- Changing page layout in Magento through XML layout

In the coming chapters, you will begin to create a Magento theme from scratch.

5
Non-default Magento Themes

As you have seen so far, it is possible to customize the basics of Magento themes such as the logo file, favicon, and changing the layouts of pages within your store. This chapter covers more advanced Magento theming techniques which you will find useful in creating a Magento theme from scratch:

- Beginning a new Magento 1.4 theme
- Customizing the header area of your store
- Customizing the general aspects of the primary content area of your store
- Customizing the footer area of your Magento store

Beginning a new Magento 1.4 theme

In Magento 1.3, you may have copy-and-pasted a theme such as the Blank theme in its entirety and then edited the various stylesheets, images, templates, and layout files required. In Magento 1.4, the altered theme hierarchy and theme structures mean that you can work in a way that is less disruptive to your Magento store when you come to update it.

The case study design

The case study theme for the M2 Store — these examples are with the aim of creating a theme suitable for Magento to accommodate this design:

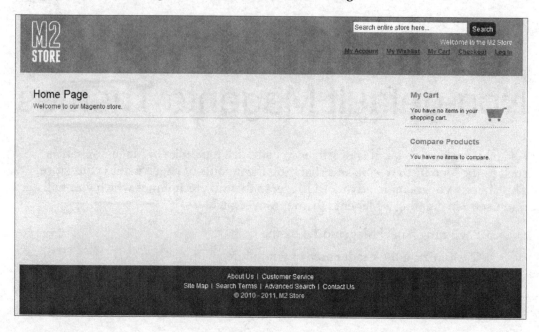

Creating new theme directories

The first step in creating the new theme is to create two new directories. Firstly, you need to create a directory to contain the new Magento theme layout and template files: as the example theme is for the M2 Store, we'll call it m2. With this in mind, you need to create a directory called /app/design/frontend/default/m2, where m2 is the name of your new theme's directory.

Theme directory name

It's best practice to name the directory for your new theme using entirely lowercase letters with no space characters (though you can use hyphens and underscores).

Within this newly created directory, you will now need to create two further directories: the /app/design/frontend/default/m2/layout directory, for layout files for our new theme and the /app/design/frontend/default/m2/template for any template files we decide to change during our Magento theme customization project.

After creating the `/app/design/frontend/default/m2/layout` directory, create a new layout file called `local.xml` (you can leave it empty for now, we'll use this shortly).

Secondly, you will need to create a directory for your new Magento theme's skin files (stylesheets and images) at `/skin/design/frontend/default/m2`. In this new skin directory, create a new file called `local.css` within another sub-directory called `/css` (again, we'll come back to this later). You may also want to create a sub-directory called `/skin/design/frontend/default/m2/images` for any associated images for your new theme at this point.

Preserving Magento theme directory hierarchy

It is important to preserve the directory structure for new Magento themes that you create so that Magento can find the relevant files of your theme where it is expecting them.

Basic local.xml layout file

Next, you will need a very basic `local.xml` file for your theme, to tell it that the `local.css` file is in the `/skin/design/frontend/default/m2/css` directory. Using the following layout XML, tell Magento that your new theme has a new stylesheet (the `local.css` file you created before) associated with it:

```xml
<?xml version="1.0" encoding="UTF-8"?>
<layout>
 <default>
  <reference name="head">
   <action method="addCss">
   <stylesheet>css/local.css</stylesheet>
   </action>
  </reference>
 </default>
</layout>
```

At this stage, you may also want to remove some of the unnecessary elements from the theme using the `remove` action of Magento's layout. For this example, remove the callouts displayed in the left and right-hand columns, and the PayPal logo:

```xml
  <default>
 <layout>
 <!-- some omitted XML from above -->
  <remove name="left.permanent.callout"/>
  <remove name="right.permanent.callout"/>
```

```
        <remove name="paypal.partner.right.logo"/>

    </default>
    </layout>
```

Enabling the new theme

You can now enable the new theme and begin customizing Magento. To enable the new theme, log in to your administration panel and navigate to **System | Configuration**:

Next, select the **Design** tab from the left, ensuring that the **Current Scope Configuration** is set to **Default Store View** (you'll find this at the top-left of your screen):

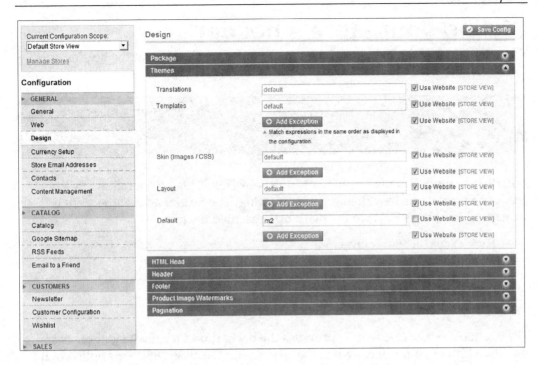

After clicking on the **Save Config** button to the top-right of the screen, refresh the frontend of your Magento store to see the new layout instructions take effect, removing the callouts and PayPal logo:

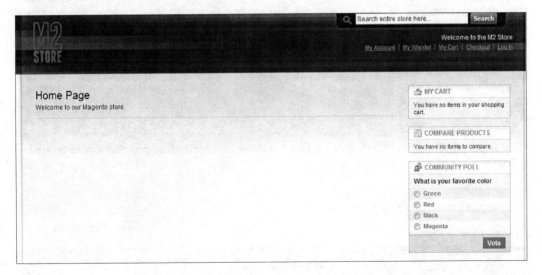

Styling your store's header

You may find it easier to begin at the top of your store's design, at the header. Currently, the store's header looks like the following:

With this is mind, you may need to change your store's logo (covered in a previous chapter) to match the new theme you're creating. The header area of the store is structured in a way similar to the mark up presented next:

```
<div class="header-container">
 <div class="header">
  <!-- header content -->
 </div><!--/end of .header-->
</div><!--/end of .header-container-->
```

The `.header-container <div>` provides the background for the header area for the full width of your screen, while the `<div>` with the class `.header` applied to it is the element that wraps the logo, search box, and account links into the centre of the screen.

Begin styling the header area by adding CSS to your new theme's `local.css` file in the `/skin/frontend/default/m2/css` directory. Start with the `.header-container` element by removing the background image and color attributes, and the dark-blue border that is applied to the top and bottom of this element:

```
.header-container {
background: none;
border-width: 0
}
```

At this point, it is also worth styling the `.header` element, changing its background color:

```
.header {
background: #f76300
}
```

Next, you will need to apply style to the `<body>` element to remove the dark blue bar still apparently present in the `.header-container` element:

```
body {
background: #f7f6f4
}
```

Once the store is refreshed, you'll see that the background surrounding the header area becomes a pale brown/grey color:

Finally for this section, you can style the logo to become slightly transparent when it is hovered over by a visitor to your store, that reinforces the idea that they're able to click on it to return to your store's homepage:

```
a.logo:hover img {
opacity: 0.6
}
```

If you now refresh your Magento store and hover over the logo, you will see that it turns slightly transparent when you hover over it:

Cross-browser support of opacity

Though the `opacity` attribute of CSS is supported in many browsers such as Opera, Firefox, Safari, and Chrome, you will find that this effect does not work in older versions of Internet Explorer.

That's the basic styling for the header of your new Magento theme complete! You can move on to styling other elements within the header area now.

Styling the user account links

Next on the list is styling the user account links that are contained within the header, at the top-right of the screen beneath the search box:

As they're in a location that is fairly common for these type of links (that is, where most customers are likely to look for them), we can leave the positioning of these as it is and concentrate on improving the contrast of the colors for our new Magento theme. With this in mind, return to your new theme's `local.css` file and continue to add style:

```
.quick-access .links a {
color: #803300;
font-weight: bold
}
  .quick-access .links a:hover {
  color: #FFF
  }
```

Here, you added CSS to change the colors of the links and dividers to a deeper orange than the background of the `.header` element you changed earlier. Just as importantly, you also changed the `:hover` state of the links in the CSS to change the links to white when a visitor to your store hovers over them, to reinforce to the visitor that they are able to interact with this portion of your Magento store.

Our next task is to remove the vertical lines between the items in the user account links. These are set as background-images on the `<li>` element in the `.quick-access <div>`:

```
.quick-access .links li {background: none}
```

If you now refresh the frontend of your Magento store, you'll see these changes take effect:

Customizing the welcome message

You can customize the welcome message, contained in the `.quick-access` element in your store's header discussed before, in Magento's administration panel. Log in to your store's administration panel and navigate to **System | Configuration** and in the **Default Store View** scope (selected from the drop-down list at the top-left of your screen), select the **Design** tab in the left-hand column:

Under the **Header** section in the main content area, change the value in the **Welcome Text** field to reflect the welcome message you want to appear on your Magento store:

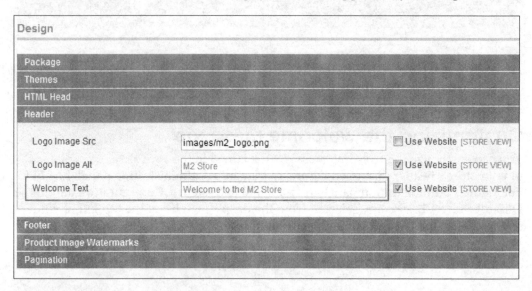

Styling the search box

The search box of your Magento store currently looks like the following:

The search box (referred to in Magento as the 'search mini form') is contained within a `<form>` element with the `id` of `search_mini_form`:

```
<form id="search_mini_form"
 action="http://www.example.com /magento/index.php/catalogsearch/
result/"
 method="get">
 <div class="form-search">
  <label for="search">Search:</label>
  <input id="search" type="text" name="q" value="" class="input-text"
/>
   <button type="submit" title="Search" class="button">
   <span><span>Search</span></span>
   </button>
   <!-- autocomplete JavaScript etc omitted -->
   </div>
</form>
```

You can style it by applying CSS in your theme's `local.css` file to elements within this id, `#search_mini_form`. Firstly, remove the background image from the `.form-search` `<div>` within the form element so that the search box integrates seamlessly with our new theme design. You can also provide a little padding for the `.form-search` element at the top, to space it away from the top of the browser window:

```
#search_mini_form .form-search {
background: transparent;
padding-top: 10px
}
```

Your progress so far should look like the following:

At this stage, you can also style the **Search** button, which is a `<button>` element with a class of `.button` applied to it:

```
#search_mini_form .button {
background: #803300;
border-radius: 5px;
color: #FFF;
padding: 5px
}
```

This CSS sets the background color a deep orange and creates rounded corners around it for those browsers which do support the `border-radius` CSS attribute. However, if you refresh your page now, you'll see that the `<button>` element still has a blue background as it does in the preceding screenshot, albeit with an orange border surrounding it:

This is because the `<button>` element makes use of two `<span>` elements nested inside it to create a cross-browser compatible, scalable search button with rounded corners, and a gradient background:

```
<button type="submit" title="Search" class="button">
 <span>
  <span>Search</span>
 </span>
</button>
```

There are two possible solutions to this:

1. You could style the `<span>` elements using CSS to remove the background images that create this effect.

2. You could edit the relevant Magento template file to remove the superfluous `<span>` elements from your Magento theme's markup.

Here, you can take the second option to explore Magento's templates in more detail.

Customizing a Magento template file

This is a point at which you will need to break away from editing Magento's skin files to customizing Magento's template files. Firstly, you will need to identify the template that provides the mini search form's markup for Magento: you may want to make use of Magento's template path name feature.

Template path name feature refresher

Log in to your Magento administration panel and navigate to **System | Configuration**. Ensure that you are in the **Default Store View** scope and not the **Default Config** scope. In the **Developer** tab, expand the **Debug** section and set **Template Path Hints** to **Yes**, and then click on **Save Config**.

There is a more detailed guide to this feature in a previous chapter.

Now that template paths hints are enabled, refresh your Magento store's frontend and look at the value presented for the mini search form:

The value displayed in the red box now visible is `frontend/base/default/ template/catalogsearch/form.mini.phtml`. Copy this file into your new theme's template directory (that is, `/app/frontend/default/m2/template/ catalogsearch/form.mini.phtml`). Now open the file for editing, and locate the line that reads:

```
<button
 type="submit"
 title="<?php echo $this->__('Search') ?>"
 class="button">
 <span>
  <span><?php echo $this->__('Search') ?></span>
```

```
    </span>
  </button>
```

Remove the `<span>` elements from this, so that the line now reads the following:

```
<button
  type="submit"
  title="<?php echo $this->__('Search') ?>"
  class="button">
  <?php echo $this->__('Search') ?>
</button>
```

You can now save and re-upload the file to your Magento installation. If you refresh the frontend of your store, you'll see the `<button>` styled as you initially intended it to be:

That's the header of your new Magento theme complete, for now at least:

Data access methods and scopes in Magento

For more information on accessing data for use in your Magento themes, you can refer to the Magento Wiki: `http://www.magentocommerce.com/wiki/4_-_themes_and_template_customization/0_-_theming_in_magento/data_accessing_methods_from_within_various_scopes`.

Styling your store's content area

The next obvious area for you to begin to customize is the primary content area (that is, the section between your store's header and footer). Your first task is to style the areas to match more closely the header area you have just customized. At present, the content area will look much like the following:

Take a look at the structure of the HTML of this area of your store. You will see that it is basically structured like the header of your store was, with a .main-container element spanning the full width and height of the content area and a <div> with the class .main used as a wrapper around all of the content, centering this in the center of the screen:

```
<div class="main-container">
 <div class="main">
  <!-- main content area content -->
 </div><!--/end of .main-->
</div><!--/end of .main-container-->
```

Open your theme's local.css file again (remember it is located in the skin/frontend/default/m2/css directory), and remove the background-image associated with the .main-container element:

```
.main-container {
background: transparent
}
```

At this point, you can also remove the background image and color associated with the `.main` element, as for this theme the background image associated with `<body>` needs to be shown below the content:

```
.main-container,
.main {
background: transparent
}
```

If you now refresh the frontend of your Magento store again, you will see that your newly added CSS has had the desired effect:

Styling the column blocks

Your new theme is slowly starting to take shape! Your next task is to style the blocks that appear in the left and right-hand columns of your store, such as the **MY CART COMPARE PRODUCTS**, and **COMMUNITY POLL** blocks seen on the homepage:

While there are quite a large number of these, they are all contained within a `<div>` with the class `.sidebar` by default, with an additional class-`.col-right` or `.col-left` - to indicate whether the blocks appear in the right-hand or left-hand column respectively. The blocks all follow a similar HTML structure:

```
<div class="block block-name">

 <div class="block-title">
  <strong><span>(Block title)</span></strong>
 </div><!--/end of block-title-->

 <div class="">
  <!-- content of this block -->
 </div><!--/end of block-content-->

</div><!--/end of block-->
```

There are a few tasks you can do here:

1. Customize the relevant templates to make the text in the `.block-title` element more semantically valid by using `<h3>` elements instead of `<strong>`.

2. Customize the look and feel of these blocks in general (you can come back to customizing specific blocks at a later date).

Customizing the sidebar basket/cart block

Working from the top-down in the sidebar, start with the **MY CART** block:

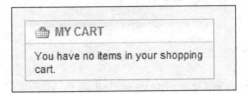

Turn on template path names in your Magento administration panel and then refresh the frontend of the store, and you will see that the file we need here is called `sidebar.phtml`, located in the `/app/frontend/base/default/template/checkout/cart` directory:

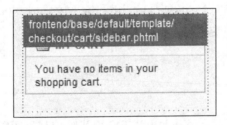

Copy the `sidebar.phtml` file and copy it to the corresponding directory in your new theme (that is, `/app/frontend/default/m2/template/checkout/cart`). Open the file and locate the line that reads:

```
<strong>
 <span>
  <?php echo $this->__('My Cart') ?>
 </span>
</strong>
```

Remove the `<strong>` and `<span>` elements, and replace them with a single `<h3>` element to wrap the PHP which outputs the name of the block (**My Cart**, in this block):

```
<h3>
  <?php echo $this->__('My Cart') ?>
</h3>
```

If you now upload the `sidebar.phtml` and refresh the frontend of your Magento store, you will see that the heading appears differently than before:

This is because `<h3>` elements are not yet styled as they should be: this will be covered later in this chapter.

Customizing the sidebar COMPARE PRODUCTS block

The **COMPARE PRODUCTS** block is below the **My Cart** block in the sidebar:

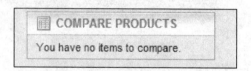

Using template path names again, you'll find that the 'compare products' block is located in the `/app/frontend/base/default/template/catalog/product/compare` directory and named `sidebar.phtml`, as was the case for the **My Cart** block:

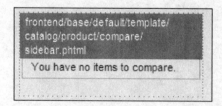

Copy-and-paste the `sidebar.phtml` into your new theme's relevant directory and begin editing it, as we did with the **My Cart** block, finding the line that reads:

```
<strong>
 <span>
  <?php echo $this->__('Compare Products') ?>
   <?php if($this->helper('catalog/product_compare')-
>getItemCount()>0): ?>
    <small>
     <?php
      echo $this->__('(%d)',
       $this->helper('catalog/product_compare')->getItemCount()) ?>
    </small>
    <?php endif; ?>
 </span>
</strong>
```

As before, replace the `<strong>` and `<span>` elements with a single `<h3>` element, leaving the `<?php>` snippets as they are, presuming that you want the number of products being compared to be saved. The new code for this line should now read:

```
<h3>
   <?php echo $this->__(<Compare Products') ?>
    <?php if($this->helper('catalog/product_compare')-
>getItemCount()>0): ?>
     <small>
      <?php
      echo $this->__('(%d)',
       $this->helper('catalog/product_compare')->getItemCount()) ?>
     </small>
     <?php endif; ?>
 </h3>
```

If you upload the file and refresh the frontend of your store, you'll see the heading's style appear in a similar style to the **My Cart** block's heading:

Customizing the sidebar poll block

In a similar way to the cart and 'compare products' sidebar blocks, you could customize the sidebar poll block's markup too.

Instead, you can make use of Magento's layout to remove the poll block from your store. Open your new theme's `local.xml` file, located in the `/app/design/frontend/default/m2/layout` directory and find the lines that read as follows, that you added previously:

```
<remove name="left.permanent.callout"/>
<remove name="right.permanent.callout"/>
<remove name="paypal.partner.right.logo"/>
```

Below the line that reads `<remove name="paypal.partner.right.logo"/>` but before the `</default>`, add this new layout instruction to remove the poll block from both your left and right-hand sidebars:

```
<remove name="right.poll"/>
<remove name="left.poll"/>
```

Upload this file to your theme's `layout` directory and refresh your Magento store's frontend to see the poll block disappear from your store's sidebar:

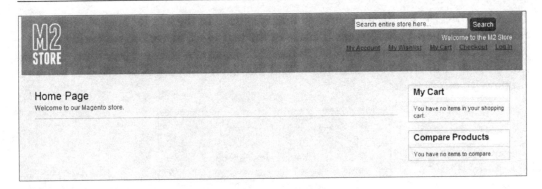

Styling the sidebar blocks

Now that you have finished altering the markup of the sidebar blocks, you can begin to style it. Return to editing your Magento theme's `local.css` file, located in the `/skin/frontend/default/m2/css` directory of your Magento installation.

Firstly, it makes sense to style the block as a whole, that is apply CSS to the `.block` elements within the `.sidebar` region. Here, you can remove the border applied all around the blocks and replace it with a dotted border 2 pixels (`2px`) wide along the bottom edge of the block, as well as applying some padding to the bottom of the block to give a greater sense of space between the elements:

```
.sidebar .block {
border-color: #b3b3b3;
border-style: dotted;
border-width: 0 0 2px 0;
padding-bottom: 5px
}
```

Next, turn to the styling of the block's headings. As you just saw, the block headings are contained within a `<div>` of class `.block-title`, so you can apply the following style to them:

```
.sidebar .block-title {
background: none;
border-bottom: none
}
.sidebar .block-title h3 {
color: #f76300;
font-size: 125%
}
```

This CSS turns the headings to orange that was used in the header area of your new Magento theme and lessens the size of the text used, as well as removing the gradient background image applied to the `.block-title` element previously. If you now refresh your store, you should see that the block titles are now styled to be more fitting with our new design:

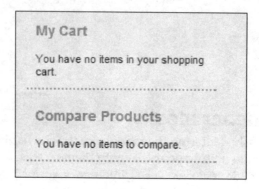

Styling a specific sidebar block

You have now styled the sidebar blocks of your Magento theme generally, but it is possible to define style specifically aimed towards a particular sidebar block if you wish. To do this, you will first need to find the class associated with the specific block in mind. In this example, you will be using the **My Cart** block, that should appear on your store's homepage (and other pages) in the right-hand column.

To find the `<div>`'s class reference we need to style it, you can use a browser 'Inspect Element', Developer Toolbar tool such as Opera's Dragonfly, Firefox's Web Developer extension, or Google Chrome's 'Inspect Element'. Failing those, you could simply look at the source of the page.

Either way, you will see that the class we need for the **My Cart** block is `.block-cart` (typically, they follow the pattern `.block-` followed by the name of the feature that the block is related to). You can now add styling specifically to this block! For this example, you will be adding a shopping cart icon to the background of the **My Cart** block. The image itself looks like the following, scaled up:

Open your theme's `local.css` file (in the `/skin/frontend/default/m2/css` directory) and add the following CSS to show the background shopping-cart image, and to give it padding to the right, so that the content isn't displayed over the background image, impairing its legibility:

```css
.sidebar .block-cart .block-content {
background: transparent url("../images/sidebar_cart_bg.png") no-repeat
right center;
padding-right: 50px
}
```

If you refresh the frontend of your Magento store after uploading the `local.css` file as well as the `sidebar_cart_bg.png` image (that needs to go in the `/skin/frontend/default/m2/images` directory) and look at the **My Cart** block, you'll now see the icon appear in the sidebar block:

Styling your store's footer

The final area of your Magento store to style for now is the footer area. You may have noticed that some of our previous changes to the theme mean that the footer area's styling has gone awry (there is no contrast between the text and the background color):

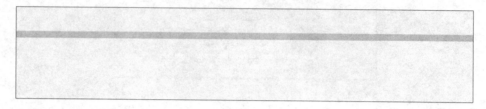

Once again editing your new theme's `local.css` file, you can go about changing this! As with the header and main content areas, the footer area is comprised of an outer 'wrapper' `<div>`, with a class of `.footer-container`, that contains another `<div>`, `.footer`, that contains the actual content in the footer area of your store.

Firstly, use CSS to remove the light-blue border along the top of the footer area and un-set the `background-color` for the full width of the screen, in-keeping with our fixed-width theme design:

```
.footer-container {
background:transparent;
border-width: 0
}
```

This is also a good time to change the color of the background to improve the contrast on the content, and to reset the padding in the `.footer` element to an even 10 pixels (`10px`) around the top, right, bottom, and left edges of the `<div>`:

```
.footer {
background: #803300;
padding: 10px
}
```

If you save and upload your `local.css` file and look at your Magento store's frontend once again, you'll see the difference you have made to the look of the footer of your store:

That's your Magento 1.4 store's footer styled basically! You can now go on to customize it more fully.

Changing the footer links

One way in which you may want to customize your store's footer is by changing the content in your store's footer. In particular, it is inadvisable to advertise the version of Magento your store is running to help avoid any potential security breaches on your store related to vulnerabilities with that version of Magento.

To change your store's footer, you need to enable template path hints in your Magento installation's administration panel to find the template file you need to edit, as you've done before. You will see that the template path hints tell us that the footer template file you're after is located in the `/app/design/frontend/default/m2/template/page/html` directory:

As with the other times you have altered your theme's template files, you will need to copy the `footer.phtml` from `/app/design/frontend/base/default/template/page/html` to your theme's template directory at `/app/design/frontend/default/m2/template/page/html`. The entirety of the file is relatively small compared to other Magento template files you may have seen:

```
<div class="footer-container">
 <div class="footer">
   <?php echo $this->getChildHtml() ?>
   <p class="bugs"><?php echo $this->__('Help Us to Keep Magento
Healthy') ?> - <a href="http://www.magentocommerce.com/bug-tracking"
onclick="this.target='_blank'"><strong><?php echo $this->__('Report
All Bugs') ?></strong></a> <?php echo $this->__('(ver. %s)',
```

```
Mage::getVersion()) ?></p>
    <address><?php echo $this->getCopyright() ?></address>
  </div>
</div>
```

The PHP statement `<?php echo $this->getChildHtml() ?>` retrieves the content associated with the footer area. You can edit this through Magento's CMS feature.

The next lines, contained within the `<p>` element with class `.bugs`, are what inserts the version of Magento into the footer, so we'll remove this. Your `footer.phtml` file should now look like the following:

```
<div class="footer-container">
 <div class="footer">
   <?php echo $this->getChildHtml() ?>
   <address><?php echo $this->getCopyright() ?></address>
 </div>
</div>
```

The remaining line, `<address><?php echo $this->getCopyright() ?></address>`, inserts the copyright notice you may have seen in the footer before:

© 2008 Magento Demo Store. All Rights Reserved.

You can edit the copyright notice's content in Magento's administration panel. Log in and navigate to **System | Configuration** and then select the **Design** tab from the left-hand side of the screen. Ensuring that the **Current Configuration Scope** is set to **Default Store View**, expand the Footer section in the primary content area to the right of your screen:

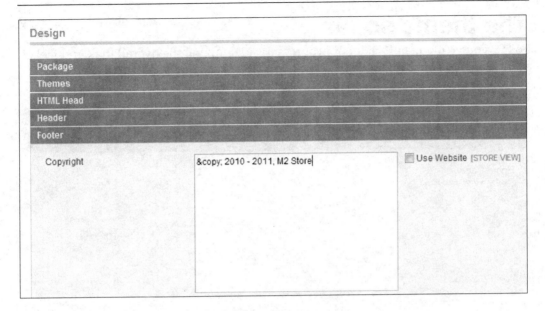

Click on **Save Config** to the top-right of the screen and then look at your store's frontend to see the new content in the footer:

Default value for the copyright notice

The default value for this is located in the `config.xml` file in Magento's `/app/code/core/Mage/Page/etc` directory but it is not recommended that you edit files in Magento's core to protect the ability to upgrade Magento more easily in the future.

The theme so far

So far, you've made quite a lot of progress in customizing the overall look and feel of your Magento store:

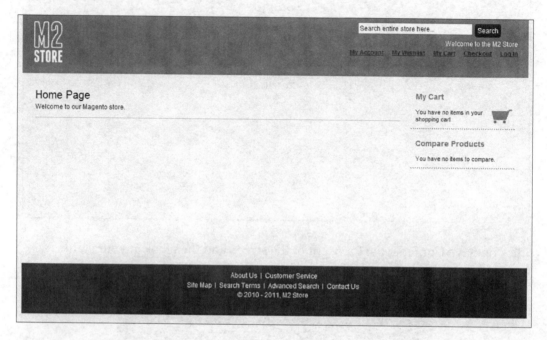

You may have noticed, however, that there's still much you can do to customize your store more fully!

Summary

In this chapter, you have begun to customize a Magento theme from scratch. In particular, you have learnt:

- How to style common elements in your Magento store's header, including:
  - The mini search form
  - Your store's logo
  - The 'quick access' user account links

- How to style the basic structural elements of the primary content area of your Magento store, including sidebar blocks such as:
  - The **My Cart** block
  - The **Compare Products** block
  - The **Community Polls** block

- How to style your store's footer area

In doing so, you have customized your theme using multiple aspects of Magento theming, such as skin changes, layout changes, and template changes. In the coming chapters, you will continue to customize your store, looking deeper into the other aspects of a Magento theme you may need to customize.

6

More Magento Theming

In the previous chapter, you began to create a custom Magento theme from the very beginning. In this chapter, you'll continue to look at theming your Magento store with various techniques, including the following:

- Integrating unusual typefaces into your Magento store using `@font-face`
- Customizing your store's product views
- Styling additional areas of your Magento store including the log in page
- Creating and customizing your store's navigation

The theme so far

If you recall, your new Magento theme, M2 currently looks like the following:

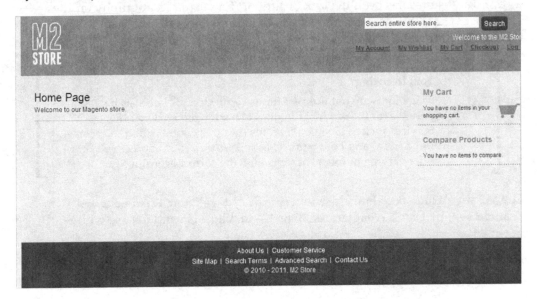

In this chapter, you will learn how to further customize your Magento 1.4 store, ending with a store that looks a little more polished:

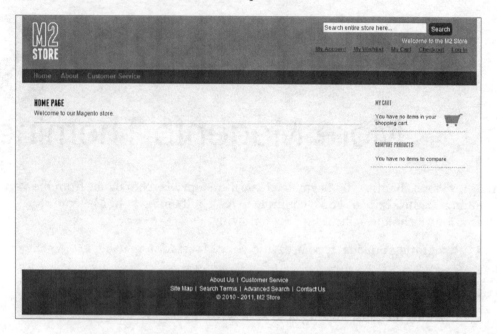

Using @font-face with Magento 1.4

For designers and developers, one of the more disappointing aspects of building websites and stores has been the lack of support for custom typography on sites. The `@font-face` CSS attribute allows you to more reliably display a specific typeface to your website visitors.

Font licensing

Many fonts are not licensed for use with `@font-face`, as it's possible for the original font files to be downloaded by others. Services such as Google Webfonts (`http://code.google.com/webfonts`) and Font Squirrel (`http://www.fontsquirrel.com`) offer varying numbers of fonts with the correct licensing.

The M2 store's logo uses Franchise font (`http://derekweathersbee.com/franchise/`) by Derek Weathersbee, which—luckily—is valid for use with `@font-face`.

Converting typefaces for @font-face

There are a number of formats for typefaces available which are used within
@font-face. Typically, you may only have a typeface in one format, such as
TrueType or OpenType. To provide as much support for your choice of typeface
as possible in your Magento store, you will want to convert to a range of formats.

There are a number of online @font-face conversion tools that generate the
necessary CSS and typeface files for you, including Font Squirrel's FontFace
Generator (http://www.fontsquirrel.com/fontface/generator).

@font-face support across browsers

There is surprisingly good support for @font-face across even older browsers.

EOT: Internet Explorer

The **EOT (Embedded Open Type)** format typefaces are supported in all versions of
Internet Explorer.

TTF: Safari, Opera, Chrome, and Firefox

Safari version 3.2 onwards, Opera version 10 onwards, Firefox version 3.5 onwards,
and all versions of Chrome support the **TTF (TrueType Format)** for typefaces in
@font-face.

OTF: Safari, Opera, Chrome, and Firefox

Similarly to the TrueType Format, **OTF (OpenType Format)** is supported by
Safari version 3.2 onwards, Opera version 10 onwards, Firefox version 3.5
onwards, and all versions of Chrome support the TTF (TrueType Format) for
typefaces in @font-face.

SVG: iPhone and Chrome

The **SVG (Scalable Vector Graphics format)** is supported by the iPhone and
Chrome browsers. SVG font files are specially formatted .svg files that contain
vector graphics for each glyph and character of the typeface it represents, allowing
for easy scalability.

WOFF: Firefox

The **WOFF (Web Open Font Format)** is currently supported by Firefox, but is in the process of becoming a standard for font formats across all major browsers, including those by Opera, Microsoft, and Mozilla.

CSS for @font-face

The CSS for using the `@font-face` attribute is relatively simple. In your new theme's `local.css` file (in the `/skin/frontend/default/m2/css` directory), add the `@font-face` CSS at the top of the file:

```
@font-face {
font-family: 'FranchiseRegular';
src: url('../types/franchise-webfont.eot');
src: local('?'), url('../types/franchise-webfont.
woff') format('woff'), url('../types/franchise-webfont.
ttf') format('truetype'), url('../types/franchise-webfont.
svg#webfontgvcdROVT') format('svg');
font-weight: normal;
font-style: normal;
}
```

 Note the order in which the various font formats are introduced into the CSS, this maximizes browser support.

Now upload the converted typeface files to the `/skin/frontend/default/m2/types` directory. Finally, you can simply reference the new `@font-face` in the `font-family` CSS attribute in your `local.css` file:

```
h1, h2, h3, h4, h5, h6 {
font-family: FranchiseRegular, sans-serif;
}
```

As the Franchise typeface uses small caps for the lowercase letters, it tends to look better in headings entirely in its uppercase format, so you could add `text-transform: uppercase` to the CSS too:

```
h1, h2, h3, h4, h5, h6 {
font-family: FranchiseRegular, sans-serif;
text-transform: uppercase
}
```

You may recall that the blocks in the right-hand column of your site had headings that you styled before to orange color, using your store's default typeface:

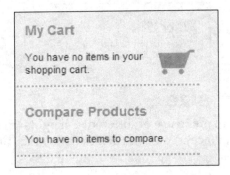

If you have saved and uploaded the changes you just made, you will now see the new typeface, Franchise, appear in headings:

Similarly, in other headings that make use of the `<h1>`, `<h2>`, `<h3>`, `<h4>`, `<h5>`, or `<h6>` element in your Magento store, this new typeface will appear. If you look at your store's homepage title, you'll remember that it used to look like the following:

Home Page
Welcome to our Magento store.

After adding the `@font-face` declaration, you should see that your heading looks like the following:

HOME PAGE
Welcome to our Magento store.

Adjusting font size

Different typefaces tend to make use of different x-heights (that is, the vertical height of characters within a typeface). You can take this into account with your stylesheet by making use of the `font-size-adjust` attribute in CSS:

```
h1, h2, h3, h4, h5, h6 {
font-family: FranchiseRegular, sans-serif;
text-transform: uppercase
font-size-adjust:0.5;
}
```

 You can find out more about the `font-size-adjust` attribute at `http://www.quackit.com/css/properties/css_font-size-adjust.cfm`.

Better results for different weights of a typeface

For more consistent results with different weights of a typeface (for example, bold-formatted text in a `<strong>` element), you may find it useful to make use of separate files for different weights. For example, if you had a bold-weighted version of the Franchise typeface, you might apply it to the `strong` element:

```
/* Define new bold-weighted font-face for Franchise */
@font-face {
font-family: 'FranchiseBold';
src: url('../types/franchisebold-webfont.eot');
```

```
src: local('?'), url('../types/franchisebold-webfont.
woff') format('woff'), url(../'types/franchisebold-webfont.
ttf') format('truetype'), url(../'types/franchisebold-webfont.
svg#webfontgvcdROVT') format('svg');
font-weight: normal;
font-style: normal;
}
h1 strong {
font-family: FranchiseBold, sans-serif;
}
```

Magento's customer account views

Alongside the product views such as category listings and the various elements of the product page, a key area you can customize in Magento is the customer account areas, which comprise of:

- The customer account log in view
- The create an account (register) view

Styling the log in view

You can navigate to the log in view of your Magento store through the 'quick access' links located at the top-right of the store by clicking on **Log In**:

As you can see, the log in view of your Magento store already has style applied from Magento's base package:

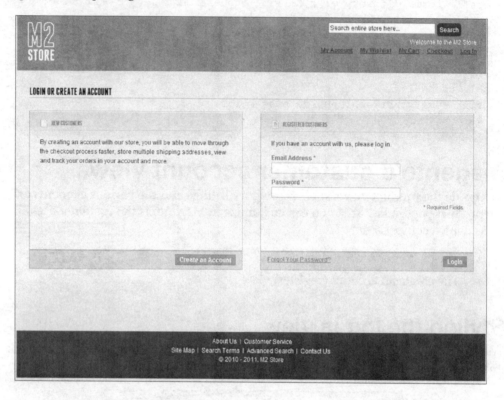

As you've done before, enable Magento's **Template Path Hints** feature in the administration panel in **System | Configuration | Developer** and you'll see that the relevant template file is in the `app/design/frontend/base/default/template/customer/form` directory and is called `login.phtml`.

Copy this file in to the `app/design/frontend/default/m2/template/customer/form` directory, and open it for editing: your aim here is to make the **Create An Account** block more obvious to customers in an attempt to increase the number of customers registering on your Magento store. Within the `login.phtml` file, locate the following lines:

```
<div class="content">
 <h2><?php echo $this->__('New Customers') ?></h2>
 <p><?php echo $this->__('By creating an account with our store,
you will be able to move through the checkout process faster, store
multiple shipping addresses, view and track your orders in your
account and more.') ?></p>
</div>
```

Add the image beneath the paragraph, enclosing it in a paragraph element of class `create-an-account-image` for easier styling in the future:

```
<div class="content">
 <h2><?php echo $this->__('New Customers') ?></h2>
 <p><?php echo $this->__('By creating an account with our store,
you will be able to move through the checkout process faster, store
multiple shipping addresses, view and track your orders in your
account and more.') ?></p>
 <p class="create-an-account-image">
  <a href="<?php echo Mage::getBaseUrl(Mage_Core_Model_Store::URL_
TYPE_WEB); ?>customer/account/create">
<img src="<?php echo $this->getSkinUrl('images/get-an-account.png');
?>" alt="Get an account" />
  </a>
 </p>
</div>
```

Note the use of the `getSkinUrl()` method: this inserts the path to the skins directory (that is, `/skin/frontend/default/m2`) into the page without you having to memorize this every time you need it.

> Using this method also ensures that you can easily copy-and-paste this file for other Magento themes you create without having to update the path to your theme's image directory.

The `getBaseUrl()` method inserts Magento's root directory into the page, to which you added the root to Magento's account registration page. Next, you need to upload an image called `get-an-account.png` into the `/skin/frontend/default/m2/images` directory:

If you now refresh the page after saving and uploading these changes, you'll see that the new graphic appears:

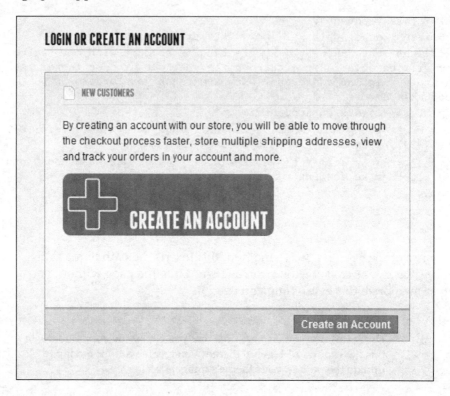

Your next task is to style these blocks to ensure greater consistency with your new theme's design. By inspecting the HTML source of the page you'll see that the two columns on this page—the **New Customers** block on the left and **Registered Customers** block on the right—are contained within a <div> of class .account-login. Each column has a class of .col-1, and then an additional class defining its purpose: .new-users and .registered-users respectively. Within these elements is a further <div> of class .content, which is where the background styling is currently applied. The **Create an Account** and **Log In** buttons at the bottom of these columns are within their own <div>s, with the class .buttons-set.

Remove the background images of these `<div>`s by applying CSS in your theme's `local.css` file in the `/skin/frontend/default/m2/css` directory and applying the color white to the background of these elements:

```
div.new-users div.content,
div.registered-users div.content,
div.new-users div.buttons-set,
div.registered-users div.buttons-set   {
background: #FFF
}
```

Once you have saved this change, refresh the page to see the newly styled blocks:

You can see that they fit your new theme's design more closely than before. Your final task here is to alter the styling applied when a customer on your store has focused on one of the fields in the **Registered Customers** block. Currently, if you apply focus to the **Email Address** field by tabbing to it on your keyboard or clicking it with your mouse, you will see that the background color changes to a pale blue:

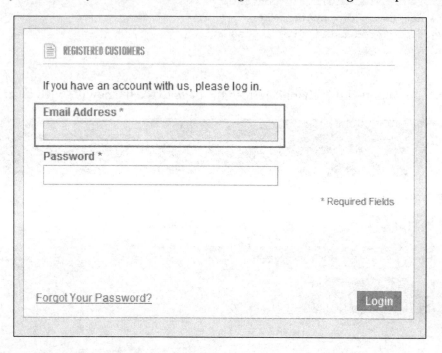

Once again, open your Magento theme's `local.css` file and apply the following code to alter the behavior of all text and password `<input>` types:

```
input[type="text"]:focus,
input[type="password"]:focus,
input[type="file"]:focus,
textarea:focus,
select:focus {
background: #fff0e7
}
```

Note that this applies the effect to most form elements across your Magento store. You can target this block specifically by editing your CSS to be more specific:

```
.registered-users input[type="text"]:focus,
.registered-users input[type="password"]:focus,
.registered-users input[type="file"]:focus,
.registered-users textarea:focus,
```

```
.registered-users select:focus {
background: #fff0e7
}
```

If you now save and upload these changes and refresh the log in view of your
Magento 1.4 store, you should see the background of the input field change to a
pale orange color when it is focused on:

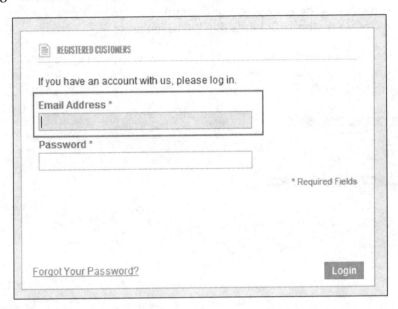

That's your store's log in view styled, though, now that you are aware of the various
components that go into styling and structuring it, you're able to customize this view
as much or little as you desire.

Remember me feature on the log in page

You can customize your Magento store to display a 'Remember Me'
option on the log in page so that visitors who enable this option are
kept logged in for longer and don't have to constantly remember their
password. There is a guide to this on the Magento website at http://
www.magentocommerce.com/boards/viewthread/196359/.

Styling the register an account view

Now that the log in view of your Magento store has been styled, you can also style your store's registration form. One easy way to navigate to this view in your store's frontend is to click the **Create an Account** button you added to Magento's log in view previously. Alternatively, navigate your browser to `http://www.example.com/magento/customer/account/create/`, if your Magento installation is in the `/magento` directory of the `example.com` domain. You will see that the **Create an Account** view of your store still looks like the base theme.

You will see that the relevant Magento template file is called `register.phtml` in the `app/frontend/base/default/template/customer/form/` directory if you use the template path hints tool:

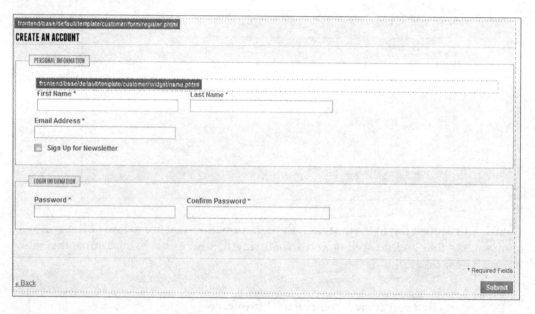

You can leave `app/design/frontend/base/default/template/customer/widget/name.phtml` as it is; this is a template file that is used to generate the **First Name** and **Last Name** fields.

At this stage you will focus on styling this view instead of editing the templates, so move on to styling these blocks as you did previously by adding CSS to your theme's `local.css` file:

```
div.fieldset {
background: #FFF
}
```

As both the **PERSONAL INFORMATION** and **LOGIN INFORMATION** forms are contained within a `<div>` with class `.fieldset`, it is relatively easy to remove the style across these elements:

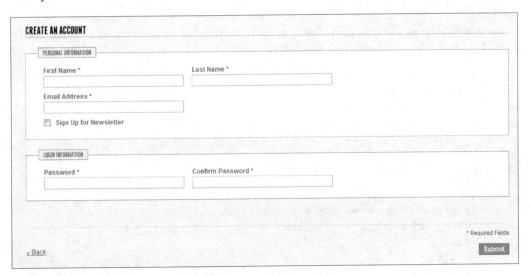

Navigation in Magento

One thing that you may have noticed that is currently missing from your Magento store is navigation. If you enable the template path hints in the administration panel, you'll see the template for navigation is in our template, but not currently displaying anything:

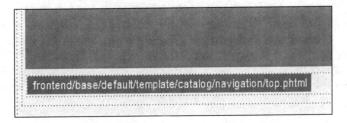

You can see that the relevant file here is located in the `/app/design/frontend/base/default/template/catalog/navigation` directory and is called `top.phtml`. You will see that the file currently looks like:

```
<?php $_menu = $this->renderCategoriesMenuHtml(0,'level-top') ?>
<?php if($_menu): ?>
<div class="nav-container">
 <ul id="nav">
```

```
    <?php echo $_menu ?>
  </ul>
</div>
<?php endif ?>
```

In your new theme, the categories are going to be displayed elsewhere in your store, so replace this file's content with the following:

```
<div class="nav-container">
 <ul id="nav">
 <li>
   <a href="<?php echo $this->getUrl('')?>">
    <?php echo $this->__('Home') ?>
   </a>
 </li>

 <li>
   <a href="<?php echo $this->getUrl('about')?>">
    <?php echo $this->__('About') ?>
   </a>
 </li>

 <li>
   <a href="<?php echo $this->getUrl('customer-service')?>">
    <?php echo $this->__('Customer Service') ?>
   </a>
 </li>

 </ul>
</div>
```

Note the use of the `getUrl()` method to insert the path to each page. If you take the Customer Service link as an example—`<?php echo $this->getUrl('customer-service')?>`—you will see that you are creating a link to the page with the URL of `customer-service`.

If you now save this file and refresh your store's frontend, you'll see the links appear in your store:

The styling for the navigation is being inherited from the base package's default interface, so you can overwrite this in the `local.css` in the `/skin/frontend/default/m2/css` directory, turning the navigation bar to a deep orange:

```
.nav-container {
background: none
}
ul#nav {
background: #803300
}
```

You can also style the link colors to be more fitting at this point:

```
#nav li a {
color: #999
}
#nav li a:hover {
color: #FFF
}
```

That's it, the navigation is styled to fit your new Magento store:

You may also find the Magento wiki useful if you want to hard-code a home link into your theme's navigation but want the remainder of the menu items to be dynamically generated within Magento: http://www.magentocommerce.com/wiki/4_-_themes_and_template_customization/navigation/add_home_link_to_menu_bar.

Hiding navigation items with CSS

You can hide navigation items with CSS by modifying Magento to associate each list-item in the menu with an id which can then be targeted with your theme's `local.css` file to be hidden using `display: none`. See Magento's wiki at: http://www.magentocommerce.com/wiki/4_-_themes_and_template_customization/catalog/hide_navigation_item_s_with_css.

Magento's product view

A fundamental view of your store that has yet to receive much attention is the product view:

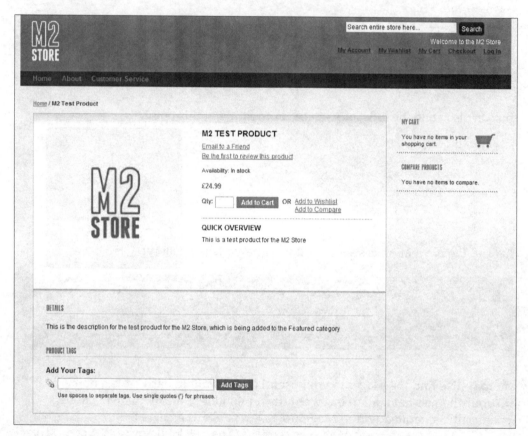

As you can see, the basic styling is fairly complete for your store's products, but as ever you can customize Magento to suit your needs. For this example, you'll remove the **Email to a Friend** feature, as well as the **Be the first to review this product** feature and add a new block to the right-hand column.

Customizing the product view template

As you saw, the first task is to remove the **Email to a Friend** option displayed beneath the product's title:

If you enable Magento's template path hints tool in the administration panel, you can see the location of the file that you need to edit in the top-right hand side of the following screenshot:

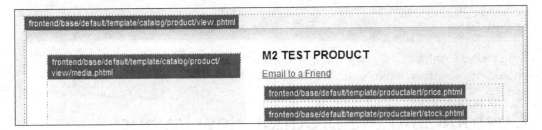

Copy-and-paste the `view.phtml` file in the `app/design/frontend/base/default/template/catalog/product` directory into the `app/design/frontend/default/m2/template/catalog/product` directory (you may need to create this if it doesn't exist already). Locate the lines that read the following and remove them:

```
<?php if ($this->canEmailToFriend()): ?>
  <p class="email-friend"><a href="<?php echo $this->helper('catalog/product')->getEmailToFriendUrl($_product) ?>"><?php echo $this->__
('Email to a Friend') ?></a></p>
  <?php endif; ?>
```

Now save this file to your Magento installation and refresh the frontend of your store in its product view and the link to **Email to a friend** should have disappeared:

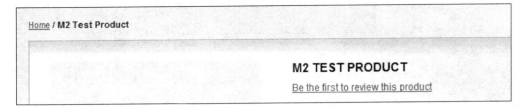

Alternatively, you could set the value of **Mage_Sendfriend** to **Disabled** in the **System | Configuration | Advanced** panel of your Magento store's administration panel; this disables the feature entirely for a theme, which may prove useful if a client does not request this feature or your theme's design does not allow for it.

Disabling Magento reviews through the CMS

You can also disable the **Be the first to review this product** feature by disabling the review feature in Magento if you're doing this: the setting you will need is called **Mage_Review** located in the **System | Configuration | Advanced** panel of your Magento administration panel. Set this value to **Disable** and refresh your cache(s) if necessary:

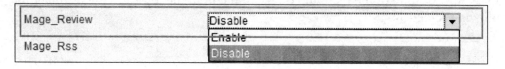

Select **Save Config** at the top-right of your screen and Magento's review feature should now be disabled in your Magento store.

Customizing the product view layout

Your next task is to remove the **COMPARE PRODUCTS** block from this page's right-hand column to simplify the product page, maximizing the impact of your store's product information and photography:

Open your theme's `local.xml` layout file and add the following lines to remove the **COMPARE PRODUCTS** block:

```
<!-- omitted layout -->
<catalog_product_view>
 <remove name="catalog.compare.sidebar"/>
</catalog_product_view>
</ layout>
```

If you now refresh the product view on the frontend of your Magento store this block will have disappeared:

Summary

In this chapter, you have looked into theming Magento in more detail and you have further customized the M2 store theme which is serving as your case study for Magento 1.4 theming:

- Making use of the `@font-face` attribute in CSS within Magento
- Styling Magento's log in and register views
- Adding and customizing navigation in Magento
- Customizing your store's product views

In the coming chapters, you will continue to delve into Magento 1.4 theming, including integrating social media elements from Twitter and Facebook into your store.

7
Customizing Advanced Magento Layout

Your Magento theme is taking shape at this point, but as before, there are still tasks you can complete to further customize your Magento store:

- Styling error messages to better help your customers when something goes wrong with your store or they find a page that no longer exists
- Styling your store's breadcrumb feature
- Creating a custom block to use in your store's layout
- Adding a Lightbox-style effect to your store's product pages
- Creating a custom `translate.csv` file to provide custom labels across your Magento store
- Adding a custom block to pages controlled through Magento's content management system (CMS)

Magento error messages and views

As a complex system, Magento displays quite a range of error messages. You can concentrate on the three messages that your customers are likely to encounter:

- The 'not found' view, shown when a customer visiting your store tries to reach a page that does not exist
- The no JavaScript error message
- The default 'note message' that informs customers about information, usually regarding an action they have just made

Customizing Magento's 404—not found view

Begin by customizing the 'not found' view in your Magento store. Firstly, navigate to a page in your Magento store that does not exist. For example, `http://www.example.com/magento/thispagedoesnotexist` should work, assuming your Magento installation is at `http://www.example.com/magento`.

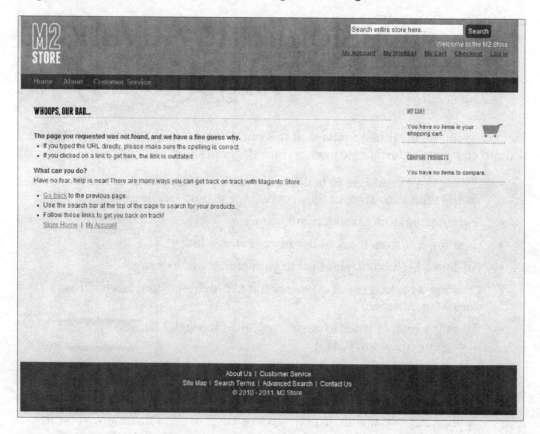

Your next step is to identify which template Magento uses to present this page; as you have done before, enable the **Template Path Hints** tool in your Magento administration panel (remember, it's located in the **System | Configuration | Developer** screen):

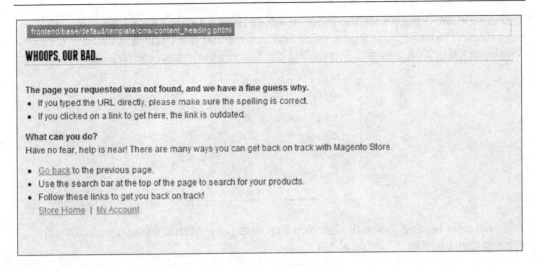

As you can see, there isn't a unique template associated with this page's structure; it relies on Magento's CMS. Remaining logged-in to your store's administration panel, navigate to **CMS | Pages** and study the list of pages that is presented:

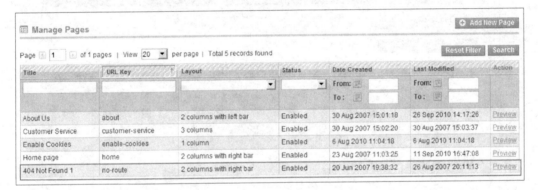

Assigning 404 error pages in Magento's CMS

You can assign a custom 404 error page in Magento's CMS by navigating to **System | Configuration | Web | CMS No Route Page** in your store's administration panel.

You should see a page with the value **404 Not Found 1** in the **Title** column (if the page doesn't exist—create a new page and ensure that the **URL Key** value is set to no-route). Click on this and then select the **Content** tab from the left-hand side:

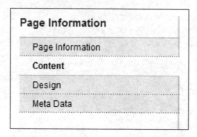

You will now be able to see the content that was present in the page, including the **Whoops, our bad** title visible above:

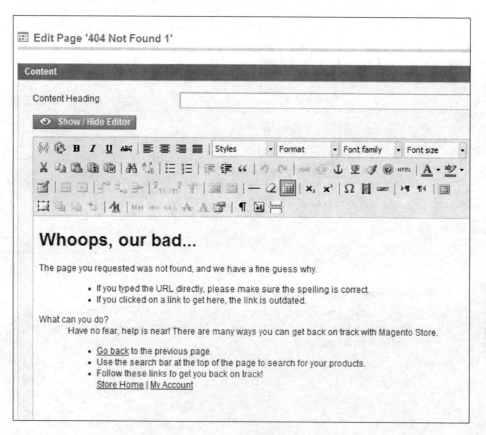

The aim for the new theme you're creating here is to create a more tailored look to your store's 'not found' error page, so now is a good time to change some of the wording if you want to and customize the look and feel of it away from that of the Default Magento theme.

Removing default values from Magento content

If you made use of Magento's default content when installing Magento, you will almost certainly want to change the words **'Magento Store'** to the name of your store!

Disable the Rich Text Editor (RTE) for the content field by clicking the **Show/Hide Editor** button. This will show the HTML that is behind the page's content.

You should now see the markup behind the page that looks like the following:

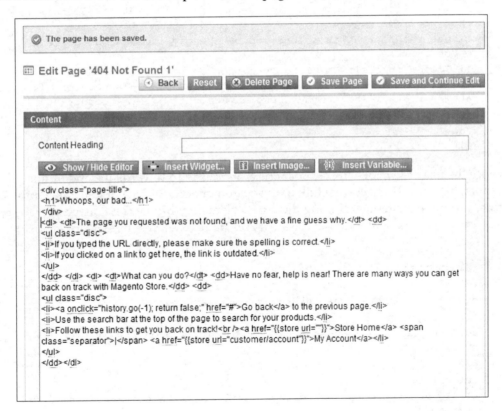

For reference, the following is the markup contained within the content field for this page by default:

```
<div class="page-title">
 <h1>Whoops, our bad...</h1>
</div>
<dl>
 <dt>The page you requested was not found, and we have a fine guess
why.</dt>
 <dd>
 <ul class="disc">
 <li>If you typed the URL directly, please make sure the spelling is
correct.</li>
 <li>If you clicked on a link to get here, the link is outdated.</li>
 </ul>
 </dd> </dl> <dl> <dt>What can you do?</dt> <dd>Have no fear, help
is near! There are many ways you can get back on track with Magento
Store.</dd> <dd>
 <ul class="disc">
 <li><a onclick="history.go(-1); return false;" href="#">Go back</a>
to the previous page.</li>
 <li>Use the search bar at the top of the page to search for your
products.</li>
 <li>Follow these links to get you back on track!<br /><a
href="{{store url=""}}">Store Home</a> <span class="separator">|</
span> <a href="{{store url="customer/account"}}">My Account</a></li>
 </ul>
 </dd>
</dl>
```

Notice the use of `{{store url="customer/account"}}` towards the end of this snippet, that inserts the correct link to the customer account area of your Magento store. Wrap the content, excluding the `<div>` element with the class of `.page-title`, in a new `<div>` element with the class `.error-page-background-image-wrapper`:

```
<div class="page-title">
 <h1>Whoops, our bad...</h1>
</div>
<div class="error-page-background-image-wrapper">
<dl>
 <dt>The page you requested was not found, and we have a fine guess
why.</dt>
 <dd>
 <ul class="disc">
 <li>If you typed the URL directly, please make sure the spelling is
correct.</li>
```

```
<li>If you clicked on a link to get here, the link is outdated.</li>
</ul>
</dd> </dl> <dl> <dt>What can you do?</dt> <dd>Have no fear, help
is near! There are many ways you can get back on track with Magento
Store.</dd> <dd>
<ul class="disc">
<li><a onclick="history.go(-1); return false;" href="#">Go back</a>
to the previous page.</li>
<li>Use the search bar at the top of the page to search for your
products.</li>
<li>Follow these links to get you back on track!<br /><a
href="{{store url=""}}">Store Home</a> <span class="separator">|</
span> <a href="{{store url="customer/account"}}">My Account</a></li>
</ul>
</dd>
</dl>
</div><!--/end .error-page-background-image-wrapper -->
```

Save these changes by clicking on the **Save Page** button at the top-right of your
screen and then open your theme's `local.css` file (located in the `/skin/frontend/`
`default/m2/css` directory) and add the following CSS:

```
.error-page-background-image-wrapper {
background: transparent url("../images/error-page-background-image-
wrapper.png") no-repeat center left;
min-height: 200px;
padding-left: 125px
}
```

You will need to create an image called `error-page-background-image-wrapper.`
`png` in your theme's `/images` directory (for example, `/skin/frontend/default/m2/`
`images`). For the M2 store, you can use this graphic:

Once you have saved and uploaded these changes, refresh the frontend of your Magento store and you should see the new styling take affect:

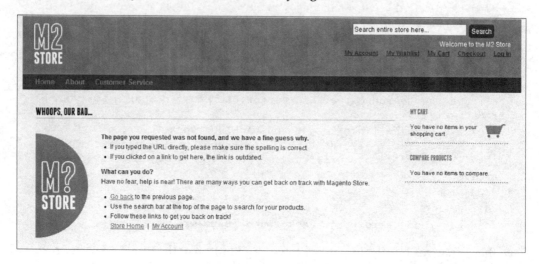

Finally, you can style the page to appear as a single column, eliminating the **My Cart** and **Compare Products** blocks displayed in the right-hand column. Return to your Magento store's administration panel and to editing the **404 Not Found 1** page in the **CMS | Pages** area, select the **Design** tab from the left-hand side:

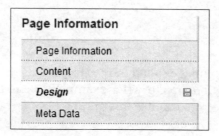

Under the **Page Layout** section here, select the **1 column** view from the drop-down for the **Layout** field:

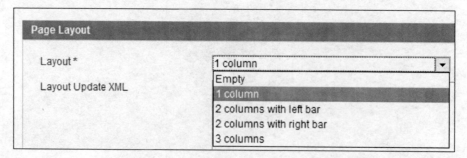

If you now click on **Save Page** once again and refresh the frontend of your Magento store, you will see the layout of the page change to accommodate its new one-column layout:

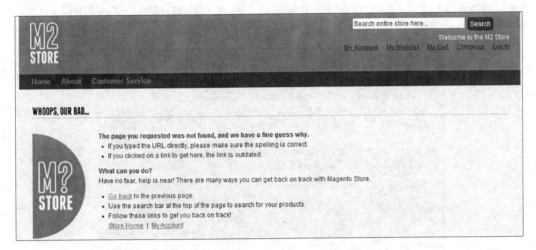

That's your store's 'not found' view customized!

The no JavaScript error message

This message is displayed on your Magento store if a visitor does not have JavaScript enabled, as parts of Magento rely quite heavily on this. By default, the message appears like the following, at the top of the store's design:

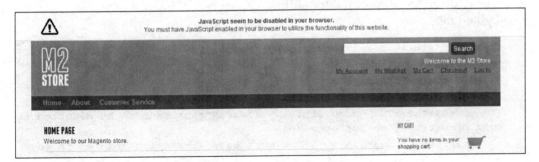

By default, it's not a particularly friendly message, so you can change this to be more welcoming for potential customers to your store. As you may have become accustomed to it by now, enable Magento's template path hints tool and refresh the frontend of your store to see the relevant Magento templates that you will need to edit:

The template path of interest to you here is the `/app/design/frontend/base/default/template/page/html/notices.phtml` file: locate this file in your Magento installation and copy it to the `/app/design/frontend/default/m2/template/page/html` directory and open it for editing; the section of interest to you is highlighted next:

```php
<?php if ($this->displayNoscriptNotice()): ?>
 <noscript>
   <div class="noscript">
    <div class="noscript-inner">
    <p><strong><?php echo $this->__('JavaScript seem to be disabled in
your browser.'); ?></strong></p>
    <p><?php echo $this->__('You must have JavaScript enabled in your
browser to utilize the functionality of this website.'); ?></p>
   </div>
   </div>
 </noscript>
 <?php endif; ?>
  <?php if ($this->displayDemoNotice()): ?>
```

```
<p class="demo-notice"><?php echo $this->__('This is a demo
store. Any orders placed through this store will not be honored or
fulfilled.') ?></p>
<?php endif; ?>
```

Replace the text within `$this->__()` statement, where they're contained within the `<noscript>` element:

```
<?php if ($this->displayNoscriptNotice()): ?>
 <noscript>
   <div class="noscript">
    <div class="noscript-inner">
    <p><strong><?php echo $this->__('Hi! JavaScript seem to be
disabled in your browser.'); ?></strong></p>
    <p><?php echo $this->__('Hi there! Welcome to the M2 Store.');
?></p>
    <p><?php echo $this->__('You will need to enable JavaScript in
your browser to use our store. If you are really stuck, you can call
us on 555 6849626 and we will do our best to help'); ?></p>
    </div>
   </div>
 </noscript>
 <?php endif; ?>
```

If you save this file and refresh your Magento store's frontend with JavaScript disabled, you'll see the new error message appear:

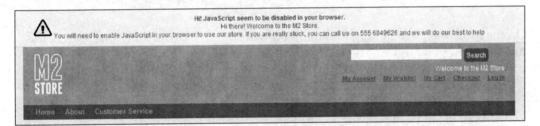

Next, you can style this error message by adding CSS to your theme's `local.css` file (again, this is located in the `/skin/frontend/default/m2/css` directory). The existing style is applied to the `div.noscript` and `div.noscript-inner` elements:

```
.noscript {
background: #ffefe4;
border-bottom: 1px #f76300 solid
}
.noscript-inner {
background-position: center 10px !important;
```

```
padding-top: 65px !important
}
```

Refresh your store's frontend to see the newly styled error message, that provides an alternate contact number for any customers without the ability to enable JavaScript:

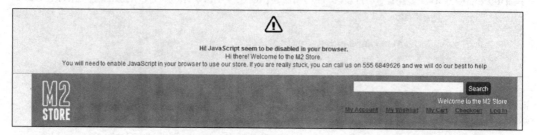

Styling the default message in Magento (.note-msg)

Finally in your spree of error and message styling for your Magento store, you can style the default message you may have seen across your Magento store. To see one appear, try to search your store for something that does not exist (for example, search for **This does not exist**):

On the resulting page in Magento that you will see after performing this search, the message that you are wanting to style will appear declaring that **Your search returns no results**:

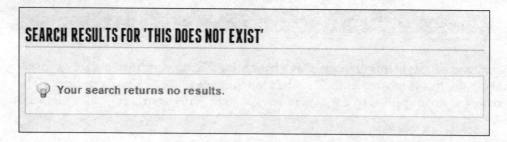

A brief inspection of the source code of this page indicates that the element we need to style in our new Magento theme's CSS file is p.note-msg. The structure in the HTML source for this message is as follows:

```
<p class="note-msg">
```

```
    Your search returns no results.
</p>
```

This defines the common structure of these messages where you see them appear in Magento. Open your theme's `local.css` file in the `/skin/frontend/default/ m2/css` directory and customize the look of these messages so it appears more consistent with the remainder of your new theme's design, while still appearing distinct from the general content of your store:

```
p.note-msg {
background: #f76300;
border: 2px #e45b00 solid;
border-radius: 10px;
color: #FFF;
padding: 10px;
text-align: center;
}
```

Now that you have changed the background and foreground colors and altered the alignment of text within the message, save and upload your new `local.css` file, and refresh the search results page you had generated earlier:

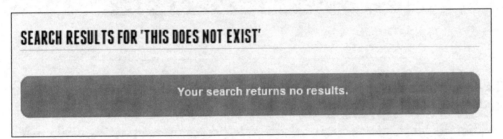

You've now made a start on styling your store's errors and messages; congratulations!

> **Displaying system errors for development sites**
>
> There is a guide on the Magento wiki which you may find useful if you want to display errors generated by your Magento store during its development: `http://www.magentocommerce.com/wiki/3_-_ store_setup_and_management/configure_magento_error_ page`.

You may also come across a 'white screen' error in Magento, which means that Magento has hit a PHP error when executing and it is unable to recover from this; the easiest remedy to this is to look in your server's error logs for the problem.

Styling your store's breadcrumb

An element you may have seen in your Magento store but which has not yet been mentioned is the breadcrumb element. To view the breadcrumb, navigate to one of the pages you linked to in the navigation towards the top of your store's design such as the **Customer Service** page. The breadcrumb is displayed below the navigation and indicates where your customer is in the structure of your website's pages:

The breadcrumb also appears on product pages, such as the following page for a product called **M2 Test Product**:

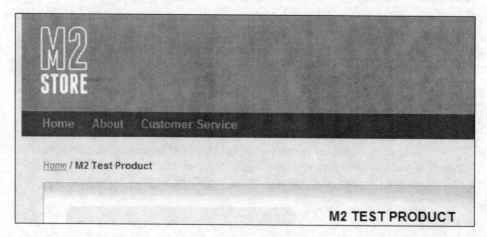

If you turn on the template path hints tool in your Magento store's administration panel and refresh the frontend view of your store, you'll see the relevant template used in Magento to define the breadcrumb:

```
frontend/base/default/template/page/html/breadcrumbs.phtml
Home / M2 Test Product
```

The Magento template file is called `breadcrumbs.phtml` and it is located in the `/app/design/frontend/base/default/template/page/html` directory. Copy the `breadrcumbs.phtml` file from this directory to your theme's own template directory (for example, `/app/design/frontend/default/m2/template/page/html`) and open it for editing:

```php
<?php if($crumbs && is_array($crumbs)): ?>
<div class="breadcrumbs">
 <ul>
 <?php foreach($crumbs as $_crumbName=>$_crumbInfo): ?>
  <li class="<?php echo $_crumbName ?>">
    <?php if($_crumbInfo['link']): ?>
    <a href="<?php echo $_crumbInfo['link'] ?>" title="<?php echo
$this->htmlEscape($_crumbInfo['title']) ?>"><?php echo $this-
>htmlEscape($_crumbInfo['label']) ?></a>
    <?php elseif($_crumbInfo['last']): ?>
    <strong><?php echo $this->htmlEscape($_crumbInfo['label']) ?></
strong>
 <?php else: ?>
  <?php echo $this->htmlEscape($_crumbInfo['label']) ?>
 <?php endif; ?>
 <?php if(!$_crumbInfo['last']): ?>
  <span>/ </span>
 <?php endif; ?>
  </li>
 <?php endforeach; ?>
 </ul>
</div>
<?php endif; ?>
```

This code essentially inserts the breadcrumb into the page as an unordered list element (<ul>) with each section of your site that is linked to it being enclosed within a list-item element (<li>). You can now customize the breadcrumbs for your Magento store by changing the slash character (/) that separates each item with an arrow character, escaped in HTML as →:

```php
<?php if($crumbs && is_array($crumbs)): ?>
<div class="breadcrumbs">
 <ul>
 <?php foreach($crumbs as $_crumbName=>$_crumbInfo): ?>
  <li class="<?php echo $_crumbName ?>">
   <?php if($_crumbInfo['link']): ?>
   <a href="<?php echo $_crumbInfo['link'] ?>" title="<?php echo
$this->htmlEscape($_crumbInfo['title']) ?>"><?php echo $this-
>htmlEscape($_crumbInfo['label']) ?></a>
   <?php elseif($_crumbInfo['last']): ?>
   <strong><?php echo $this->htmlEscape($_crumbInfo['label']) ?></
strong>
 <?php else: ?>
  <?php echo $this->htmlEscape($_crumbInfo['label']) ?>
 <?php endif; ?>
 <?php if(!$_crumbInfo['last']): ?>
 <span>&rarr; </span>
 <?php endif; ?>
  </li>
 <?php endforeach; ?>
 </ul>
</div>
<?php endif; ?>
```

If you now save and upload the breadcrumbs.phtml file and refresh your Magento store's frontend view, you should see a little arrow pointing to the right of your screen in place of the slashes used previously:

Now, you can also style the breadcrumbs by targeting `div.breadcrumbs` in your theme's `local.css` file, changing the color of the links to M2 Store's orange instead of the default blue color, and adding a little space below the breadcrumbs to create a more equal space above and below the breadcrumb:

```css
div.breadcrumbs {
padding-bottom: 12px;
}

.breadcrumbs li {
color: #666;
}
.breadcrumbs li a {
color: #f76300
}
```

After saving and uploading your changed `local.css` file, you will see the style you have just applied displayed on the breadcrumb elements:

You can also specify the breadcrumb in other template (`.phtml`) files within your Magento theme's files.

```php
<?php
  echo $this->getLayout()->getBlock('breadcrumbs')->toHtml();
?>
```

You can further customize the breadcrumb by using the `addCrumb()` function:

```php
<?php
$breadcrumbs = $this->getLayout()->getBlock('breadcrumbs');
$breadcrumbs->addCrumb('home', array('label'=>Mage::helper('
cms')->__('Home'), 'title'=>Mage::helper('cms')->__('Home'),
'link'=>Mage::getBaseUrl()));
```

```
echo $this->getLayout()->getBlock('breadcrumbs')->toHtml();
?>
```

The `addCrumb()` function takes the following parameters:

- The internal name of the crumb (`Home`, in the previous example)
- An array containing:
  - The text that is displayed between the `<a>` elements (`label`)
  - The `title` of the link, assigned to the `title` attribute within the link element
  - A value for the `link`, which is the destination of the breadcrumb (that is, the URL of this page within the breadcrumb)

Adding JavaScript into your Magento theme: Lightbox-style effects to Magento's product page

A technique you will doubtless find useful when you begin to customize your Magento themes more heavily is the ability to add JavaScript files for use in your store. A good example of this is the addition of Lightbox-style pop-ups for the photographs used on your store's product pages.

Adding a JavaScript file using Magento layout

The first task in adding Lightbox to your Magento store is to include the necessary JavaScript files. Luckily, Magento allows you to do this through layout files.

Alternate method

You could also copy the base theme's `head.phtml` file from the `/app/design/frontend/base/default/page/html` directory into the corresponding directory in your theme and include the JavaScript within the `<head>` element there, but the layout method used before is cleaner and less likely to cause headaches when updating Magento.

Download Lightbox2 from `http://www.huddletogether.com/projects/lightbox2/` and save the JavaScript files included into the `/js` directory. Save the `lightbox.css` file in your theme's `/skin/frontend/default/m2/css` directory and then save the images in the `/skin/frontend/default/m2/images` directory.

Open your theme's `local.xml` file, located in the `/app/design/frontend/default/` `m2/layout` directory, and open it for editing.Using a Magento layout `<action>` element with the method attribute set to `addJs`:

```
<catalog_product_view>
 <reference name="head">
  <action method="addJs">
    <script>lightbox/lightbox.js</script>
  </action>
 </reference>
</catalog_product_view>
```

Note that you can specify that these files only load in Magento product pages through the use of Magento layout handles (`<catalog_product_view>`), as this is the only location it's required in your store. The `name=head` attribute in the `<reference>` element tells Magento to apply the action to the `<head>` element of your Magento store.

 You only need to add the `lightbox.js` file here, as Magento includes `prototype.js` and `scriptaculous.js` by default.

Next, you will need to include the relevant CSS file to style the Lightbox:

```
<catalog_product_view>
 <reference name="head">
  <action method="addJs">
    <script>lightbox/lightbox.js</script>
  </action>
  <action method="addCss">
   <stylesheet>css/lightbox.css</stylesheet>
  </action>
 </reference>
</catalog_product_view>
```

Editing the product template file to include Lightbox

The next task is to alter the relevant product template to ensure that the Lightbox is activated when the image is clicked. If you enable template path hints once again when viewing a product page in your store, you will see that the template that controls the product photograph is called `media.phtml` in the `/app/design/frontend/base/default/template/catalog/product/view` directory:

As usual, copy-and-paste the file into your theme's own `/template` directory (for example, `/app/design/frontend/default/m2/template`) and open it to edit, locating the following line:

```
<p class="product-image">
 <?php
  $_img = '<img src="'.$this->helper('catalog/image')->init($_
product, 'image')->resize(265).'" alt="'.$this->htmlEscape($this-
>getImageLabel()).'" title="'.$this->htmlEscape($this-
>getImageLabel()).'" />';
  echo $_helper->productAttribute($_product, $_img, 'image');
 ?>
</p>
```

Wrap an `<a>` element around the `<img>` element generated here, so that it links to a large version of the image, resized to 500 pixels wide (note the use of `resize(500)` here):

```
<p class="product-image">
 <?php
  $_img = '<a rel="lightbox" href="'.$this->helper('catalog/
image')->init($_product, 'image')->resize(500).'" title="'.$this-
>htmlEscape($_product->getName()).'">
   <img src="'.$this->helper(<catalog/image>)->init($_product,
<image>)->resize(265).'" alt="'.$this->htmlEscape($this-
>getImageLabel()).'" title="'.$this->htmlEscape($this-
>getImageLabel()).'" />
   </a>';
  echo $_helper->productAttribute($_product, $_img, 'image');
 ?>
</p>
```

Note the use of `rel="lightbox"` applied to the `<a>` element here, which instigates the use of the Lightbox pop-up if a visitor clicks on the image and has JavaScript enabled. Also beware that the link's `title` attribute is used as the value for the image's caption in the pop-up (in the preceding example the name of the product is inserted).

You may also want to apply this technique to the preceding code that is applied to the image generated within `<p class="product-image product-image-zoom">`.

Once you have saved and uploaded this, click the product photograph on your product page to see the pop-up effect, assuming that you have JavaScript enabled in your browser:

No pop-up?

If the pop-up doesn't appear, double-check whether the source code of your Magento page makes use of `rel="lightbox"` correctly and ensure that the JavaScript files are in the correct directory; otherwise your store may be using a different type of product and you will need to change another section of the `media.phtml` template file as before. The spacing and line breaks within the PHP are also important; you may need to remove line breaks between the lines to see the PHP function correctly.

Changing image paths in the JavaScript file

You may have noticed that there's a missing image in the bottom-left of the pop-up. This is defined in the `lightbox.js` file you saved in the `/js/lightbox` directory previously; open `lightbox.js` for editing and locate the following lines:

```
fileLoadingImage:          'images/loading.gif',
fileBottomNavCloseImage: 'images/closelabel.gif',
```

You will need to change these values to reflect the absolute path to your theme's /
`images` directory (the following example assumes your Magento installation is in
the `/magento` sub-directory, for example `example.com/magento`):

```
fileLoadingImage: '/magento/skin/frontend/default/m2/images/loading.
gif',
fileBottomNavCloseImage: '/magento/skin/frontend/default/m2/images/
closelabel.gif',
```

You can now re-upload this file and refresh the page, and then activate the product
image pop-up again to see the close button appear correctly:

That's it, you've installed the Lightbox2 effect for your store!

Lightbox extensions for Magento 1.4

There are a number of Lightbox extensions for Magento 1.4 too, including Magento
Easy Lightbox, for which you can find the Magento Connect Key at `http://www.`
`magentocommerce.com/magento-connect/TemplatesMaster/extension/1487/`
`magento-easy-lightbox`.

Adding a conditional stylesheet for Internet Explorer in Magento

As you have seen, you can use Magento layout files to insert custom CSS files on a per-view basis across your store. Magento also allows you to add conditional stylesheets in to your theme to target various inconsistencies and bugs in Internet Explorer.

Once such inconsistency you may want to correct for earlier versions of Internet Explorer (specifically, version 6 or less) is its inability to correctly display images in the PNG (.png) format. By replacing any background images used with a GIF (.gif) file, you can retain the transparency in an image to maintain the experience of your store for as many visitors as possible.

 There are JavaScript fixes available for this such as IE PNG Fix (http://www.twinhelix.com/css/iepngfix/), but this fix, although possibly a little cumbersome, works regardless of whether or not your store's visitor has JavaScript enabled in their browser.

If you recall, in an earlier chapter you set a background image on the shopping cart block displayed to the right-hand side of your store's theme. This image was in PNG format and made use of transparency to ensure it was easier to change the store's color scheme if you wanted to in the future. As such, this is a good example to demonstrate the use of conditional stylesheets in Magento.

Your first task is to create a .gif version of the image; for this to work well, it is best to alias the image against the pale orange color you used in the background of your Magento theme (as applied to the <body> element):

Save this image in your theme's /images directory (for example, /skin/frontend/default/m2/images) as sidebar_cart_bg-ie.gif.

Creating a new stylesheet for a previous Internet Explorer version

Create a new CSS file in your Magento theme's /css directory (for example, /skin/ frontend/default/m2/css) called ie6.css and add the following CSS to replace the background image in the shopping cart block with the .gif version you just created:

```
.sidebar .block-cart .block-content {
background-image: url("../images/sidebar_cart_bg-ie.gif");
}
```

You do not need to define the background-repeat, background-color, or background-position attributes as they're already defined in your theme's local. css file: you simply need to overwrite the background-image attribute for IE6 here.

Options for IE testing your Magento store

If you don't have previous versions of Internet Explorer installed, you can install a program called IETester from http://www.my-debugbar. com/wiki/IETester/HomePage to concurrently run multiple versions of Internet Explorer on your PC. IETester does have some limitations, so be sure to read the details on the website above before using it!

Using Magento layout to specify a conditional stylesheet

The next task ahead of you is to tell Magento to load the new stylesheet you created for IE6. Open your theme's local.xml file and add the following Magento layout action within the <default> handle:

```
<default>
 <!-- other layout -->
<reference name="head">
 <action method="addItem">
  <type>skin_css</type>
  <name>css/ie6.css</name>
  <params/><if>IE 6</if>
 </action>
 <!-- other layout -->
 </reference>
</default>
```

Save and upload this file to your Magento installation and view the frontend of your Magento in Internet Explorer 6:

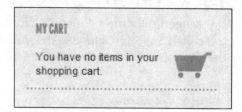

Without the use of the conditional stylesheet and the GIF, this section of your Magento store would look similar to the following screenshot in Internet Explorer 6 and below (note the different shade of grey surrounding the cart icon):

If you look in the source of the page, you'll see that the corresponding HTML is added to your theme's `<head>` element:

```
<!--[if IE 6]>
<link rel="stylesheet" type="text/css" href="http://www.example.com /
magento/skin/frontend/default/m2/css/ie6.css" media="all" />
<![endif]-->
```

Adding a new block to your Magento theme

The default layout and templates that Magento 1.4 provides are fairly comprehensive, but there are undoubtedly times that you will want to create a new block to your Magento theme. For example, you may want to add a block showing some of your suppliers' logos above the footer:

While you could just edit your theme's `footer.phtml` file in the `/app/design/frontend/default/m2/template` directory, it makes sense to create a new template block for this content. For example, if you decided to move the supplier logos to another position within your store in the future you would be able to move this with ease with Magento layout.

Creating a static block in Magento's CMS

Log in to your Magento installation's administration panel and navigate to **CMS | Static Blocks**:

Click the **Add New Block** button to the top-right of your screen:

Populate the **Block Name** and **Identifier** fields, and ensure that the **Status** field is set to **Enabled**:

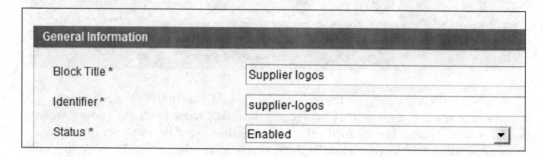

Next, you will need to populate the **Content** field by inserting some supplier logos using the Rich Text Editor provided with Magento's CMS. Click on the 'insert image' icon (an image of a tree):

A pop-up will now appear to allow you to select the image you want to insert into this static block, click the icon that appears next to the text input for the **Image URL** field:

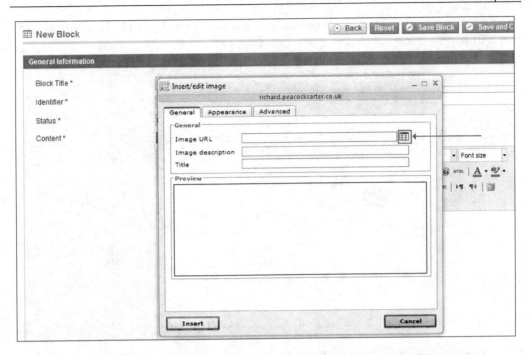

Another pop-up will now appear over the original; close the original pop-up and click on the **Browse Files** button, and select the files you want to use for the supplier logo block:

Once you have selected the files you wish to use, select the **Upload Files** button and you will see the image(s) that you uploaded appear:

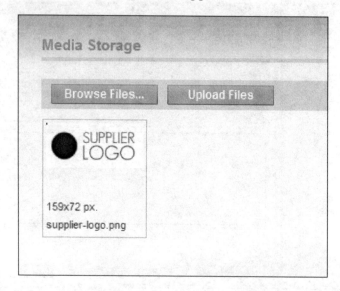

Close this pop-up and return to the editor screen for this static block, and again click on the 'insert image' icon in the Rich Text Editor. Once again, click the icon next to the **Image URL** field and then select the image(s) you want to use by clicking on them, and clicking the **Insert File** button to the top-right of the pop-up:

You're now returned to the initial pop-up and Magento has populated the **Image URL** field for you. Complete the **Image description** and **Title** fields, and click on the **Insert** button in the bottom-left of the pop-up:

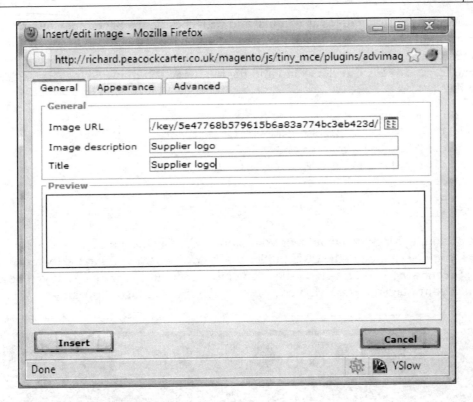

Your image will now be displayed in the **Content** field:

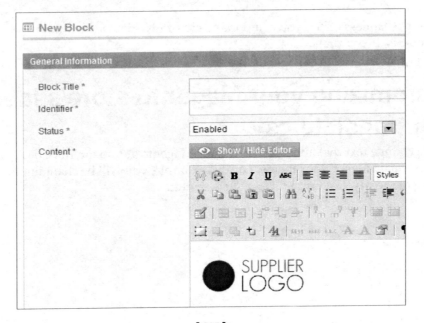

Add as many supplier logos as you like and then click on the **Save Block** button at the top-right of the screen to save the changes you have just made. Now open your Magento theme's `local.xml` file (for example, in the `/app/design/frontend/default/m2/layout` directory) and add the following layout inside the `<default>` handle:

```
<reference name="footer">
 <block type="cms/block" name="affiliates" before="-">
 <action method="setBlockId">
  <block_id>supplier-logos</block_id>
 </action>
 </block>
</reference>
```

The preceding Magento layout tells your store to display the `supplier-logos` block you just created in the CMS (notice the `type="cms/block"`) in the footer area (`<reference name="footer">`) above any other content (`before="-"`). If you now look at your Magento store's footer, you'll see the supplier logos appear:

For a more seamless effect, you could make use of PNG images with transparent backgrounds, if you prefer.

Customizing your Magento store's labels with translate.csv

You can change text that appears across your Magento's store interface by creating a custom locale file for your theme. For this example, you will be changing the wording of the **My Account** link to **Your Account**:

Open the `/app/design/frontend/default/m2/locale/en_US` directory of your Magento installation, where `en_US` is the ISO code for your store's language (you may need to create this directory if it does not exist). Create a file called `translate.csv` and add the following content to it:

```
My Account, Your Account
```

You can also add 'translations' or alterations for the remaining links' labels in this block too, by adding further lines:

```
My Account, Your Account
My Wishlist, Your Wishlist
My Cart, Your Cart
```

Note that the original value of the label is on the left, and the new value for the label is on the right after the comma. Save this file to your Magento installation's `/app/design/frontend/default/m2/locale/en_US` directory and refresh the frontend of your store to see the change take effect:

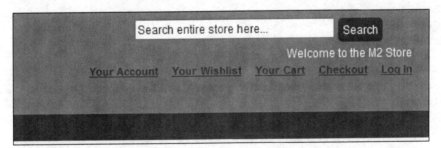

Can't see the changes?

If you can't see this change, ensure that you have configured your Magento store to display the M2 theme's locale in **System | Configuration | Design**. You will also need to ensure that the relevant cache is disabled in your administration panel in **System | Cache Management**.

Note that the preceding example will affect only the labels in stores that have been assigned the M2 locale in your Magento administration panel. If you wish to affect the labels of all of the stores managed by your Magento installation, you will need to edit the files in the `/app/locale` directory.

Adding a custom block to Magento CMS pages

At times in Magento, it can be useful to add custom blocks to your theme. To do this, open your Magento installation's administration panel and navigate to the page you wish to add the custom block to in **CMS | Pages** (in this example, use the **About** page with a left-column layout). In the **Design** tab, add this layout to the **Layout Update XML** field:

```
<reference name="left">
 <block type="core/template" name="our-address" as="our-address"
template="page/address.phtml"/>
</reference>
```

You now need to create a Magento template file called `address.phtml` and save it in the `/app/design/frontend/default/m2/template/page` directory of your installation. Provide some content for this file in the form of your store's address:

```
<h2>M2 Store's Address</h2>
<p>
M2 Store <br />
A Street <br />
A City <br />
United Kingdom
</p>
```

If you refresh your store's frontend now, you will see the address appear in the left-hand column:

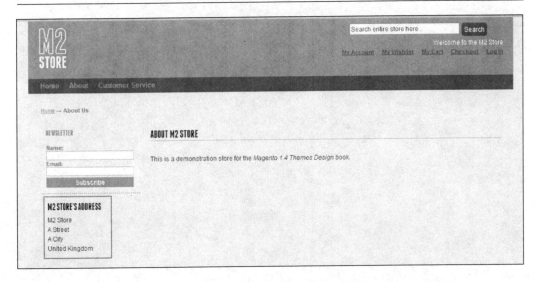

That's it, you've inserted a new custom block into your Magento theme!

Summary

In this chapter, you have further customized your new Magento theme, using a combination of Magento skin files, layout files, and template files. In particular, you have looked at the following:

- Adding a new static block through the CMS for integration within your Magento theme
- Using conditional comments for Internet Explorer-specific styling
- Styling and customizing your store's breadcrumb trail
- Installing Lightbox2 for your Magento theme
- Styling error messages and the error page
- Customizing your Magento store's label text with a `translate.csv` file
- Adding a custom block to a page controlled by Magento's CMS

In the coming chapters, you will look at styling your Magento store for print, integrate social media elements from Twitter and Facebook, and style Magento's e-mail templates.

Magento E-mail Templates

8

Now that your Magento store's theme is beginning to take shape, you can focus on another aspect of Magento that requires customizing before you can launch your store: e-mail templates. In this chapter, you will see how to:

- Edit transactional e-mail templates in your store
- Customize templates for Magento's own newsletter system
- Integrate popular e-mail newsletter systems in your Magento theme: Campaign Monitor
- Test your e-mail templates

Transactional e-mail templates in Magento

Transactional e-mail templates in Magento are sent to your customers at various events in their buying process from your store. There are over 30 transactional e-mail templates in Magento that you can customize, and what you learn next can be applied throughout these e-mail templates.

An alternative to managing these e-mail templates through Magento's default administration area is to use an extension such as **E-mail Templates Manager** (http://www.magentocommerce.com/magento-connect/AITOC%2C+Inc./extension/2117/e-mail-templates-manager) and the **Email Template Adapter** extension (http://www.magentocommerce.com/magento-connect/Finn/extension/1692/email-template-adapter).

Adding a new transactional e-mail template in Magento

Log in to your store's administration panel and navigate to **System | Transactional Emails**:

Click the **Add New Template** button at the top-right of your screen:

You will now see a new form which allows you to add a custom transactional e-mail; here you will customize the **New Invoice** template, so select the **New Invoice** value from the **Template** field and click on the **Load Template** button and wait for the template to load. Once it has loaded, you should see the contents of the template loaded in the **Template Content** field:

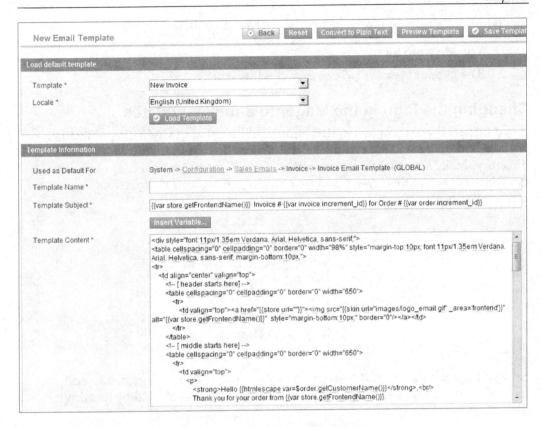

Previewing an e-mail template in Magento

Before you make any changes, you can preview the template in the browser by
clicking the **Preview Template** button at the top-right of the screen:

You'll notice there are a few things you need to change here:

1. The Magento logo.
2. The support@example.com e-mail address.

Changing the logo in the Magento e-mail templates

If you inspect the markup generated here, you'll see that the logo file points to a file named logo_email.gif in the /skin/frontend/default/default/images directory. Make sure that your theme's /skin/frontend/default/m2/images directory exists and then create and save the logo file you want to use as logo_email.gif there:

Save and upload the file and then preview the e-mail template again, also edit the path to the image file in the template's **Template Content** field by locating the following line:

```
<td valign="top">
 <a href="{{store url=""}}">
  <img src="{{skin url="/images/logo_email.gif" _area='frontend'}}"
alt="{{var store.getFrontendName()}}"  style="margin-bottom:10px;"
border="0"/>
 </a>
</td>
```

Alter this line to match the following markup that tells Magento to look in the M2 Store's images directory for the logo image:

```
<td valign="top">
 <a href="{{store url=""}}">
  <img src="{{skin url="../m2/images/logo_email.gif" _
area='frontend'}}" alt="{{var store.getFrontendName()}}"
style="margin-bottom:10px;" border="0" />
 </a>
</td>
```

You should now see your new e-mail template logo appear when you preview your template:

Variables in e-mail templates

Magento's transactional emails support quite a vast list of variables from your store that can be inserted into your store's e-mail templates. When editing the **Template Content** field, you can insert these custom fields by clicking on the **Insert Variable** button, that displays a pop-up of all available variables in your store:

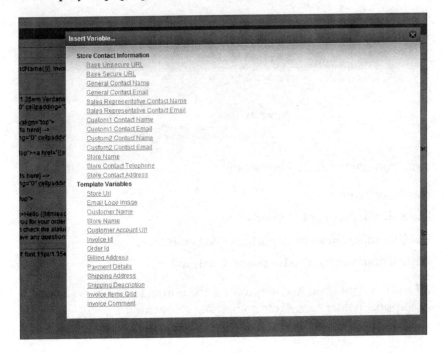

The support@example.com e-mail address displayed in this template is one of these variables: look in your template's content for the following lines:

```
<a
 href="mailto:{{config path='trans_email/ident_support/email'}}"
style="color:#1E7EC8;">
{{config path="trans_email/ident_support/email"}}
</a>
```

The variable for this e-mail address is inserted with the {{config path='trans_email/ident_support/email'}} statement (used twice). To update this variable, navigate to **System | Configuration** in your Magento store's administration panel and then select the **Store Email Addresses** navigational tab to the left-hand side of your screen:

Here you can configure e-mail addresses for:

- The **Store** owner
- The **Sales** department of your store
- The **Customer Support** department for your store
- Two custom values, **Custom1** and **Custom2**

The e-mail address you need to configure for the e-mail template is defined in the **Customer Support** field; change it to something relevant:

Now click on the **Save Config** button and return to your e-mail template (**System | Transactional Emails**) and preview it to see the change:

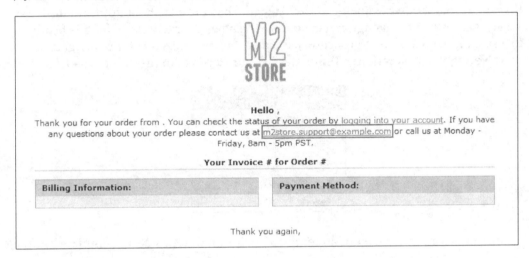

Custom variable fields

If you want to create a custom variable field for use in your store's e-mail templates, navigate to **System | Custom Variables** in your Magento administration panel.

Using the Template Styles field

Magento provides a Template Styles field where you are able to insert your custom style in the form of CSS to customize the look of the e-mail templates in your store.

Remember that, for CSS-based styles to work in HTML newsletters for many webmail and e-mail programs, you will need to include style inline in HTML elements. For example, to turn a link black, you would use the style attribute to define the color on the <a> element:

```
<a
 href="http://www.example.com"
 style="color: #000">
```

```
    Linking text
</a>.
```

Customizing Magento newsletter templates

The additional use for e-mails in your Magento store is in the form of HTML newsletter campaigns sent to customers reminding them of regular offers or informing them of the latest news from your store. Magento has this facility built-in and this system allows you to manage and customize the newsletter templates for this feature in a similar manner to the transactional e-mails you customized before. Navigate to your **Newsletter | Newsletter Templates** in your store's administration panel:

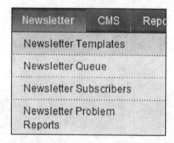

Similar to the transactional e-mail templates, click on the **Add New Template** button:

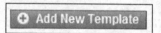

After this, a form will appear allowing you to begin creating your new HTML newsletter template in your Magento store's system. Fill in the fields for the **Template Name**, **Template Subject** (this will appear in the e-mail's subject heading once sent), **Sender Name** (this will usually appear in the e-mail's 'from' field), and **Sender Email** (this is the e-mail address the newsletter is sent from; it is best practice to make this an e-mail address from the same domain your store is located on):

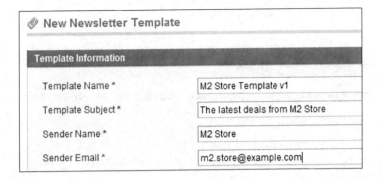

You can now focus on the **Template Content** field, unlike Magento's transactional e-mails, here you are able to use 'raw' HTML to create a visually rich newsletter template for your store.

 It's advisable to disable Magento's content editor here by clicking on the **Show / Hide Editor** button, as this can sometimes interfere with the HTML you're trying to create!

You will see that an unsubscribe link is already present in the otherwise blank template:

```
<!-- This tag is for unsubscribe link  -->
<p>Follow this link to unsubscribe
  <a href="{{var subscriber.getUnsubscriptionLink()}}">{{var
subscriber.getUnsubscriptionLink()}}</a>
</p>
```

In some countries, it is illegal to prevent your newsletters' recipients from unsubscribing and you must be careful about how you collect the e-mail addresses. For example, only customers who actively 'opt-in' to your newsletter should be receiving it.

You are able to paste in custom HTML templates used in other systems and customize the fields displayed through the **Insert Variable** pop-up. For this example, you will include a new discount offer for a particular product and the store's logo with the HTML looking similar to the following:

```
<table width="600" style="font-family: arial, verdana, sans-serif">
<tr>
 <td>
  <a href="{{store url=""}}"><img src="{{skin url="../m2/images/logo_
email.gif" _area='frontend'}}" alt="{{var store.getFrontendName()}}"
style="margin-bottom:10px;" border="0"/></a>
 </td>
```

```
</tr>
<tr>
 <td>
  <h1>20% off at M2 Store</h1>
  <p>
   Receive 20% all of our products until 1st March 2012!
  </p>
 </td>
</tr>
<tr style="background: #EFEFEF;color: #666;padding: 5px">
 <td style="font-size: 75%">
  <p>Copyright M2 Store</p>
  <!-- This tag is for unsubscribe link  -->
  <p>Follow this link to unsubscribe <a href="{{var subscriber.getUnsu
bscriptionLink()}}">{{var subscriber.getUnsubscriptionLink()}}</a></p>
 </td>
</tr>
</table>
```

Of course, you can customize your store's newsletter template to be as complex as you like! If you preview this template through the Magento administration template, you'll see the beginning of your customization:

20% off at M2 Store

Receive 20% all of our products until 1st March 2012!

Copyright M2 Store

Follow this link to unsubscribe

Guide to HTML newsletter design

For more information on designing cross-browser and e-mail platform compatible HTML newsletter templates, see the Campaign Monitor website at http://www.campaignmonitor.com/resources/.

Integrating external HTML newsletter systems with Magento

As you saw previously, the additional use for e-mails in your Magento store is in the form of HTML newsletter campaigns sent to customers reminding them of regular offers or informing them of the latest news from your store.

In addition to Magento's built-in HTML newsletter system, there are many third party newsletter systems which may provide a better level of customization or (in the case of systems such as Campaign Monitor) an additional stream of revenue for you as a web designer or web developer. You will discover how to embed two of the more popular systems—Campaign Monitor and MailChimp—into your Magento store's theme.

Integrating Campaign Monitor in your Magento store

A popular third party newsletter system is Campaign Monitor (`http://www.campaignmonitor.com`). Campaign Monitor provides a hosted e-mail newsletter system which manages subscribers, templates, and reporting:

There is a Magento extension for Campaign Monitor that you can use, but you can add the subscription box in place of Magento's newsletter system subscription form, which should be more update-proof than an extension. Enable the template path hints tool in your Magento store's administration panel and view a page that contains the newsletter block (by default, it appears in the left-hand column). If you refresh the frontend view of your Magento store, you will be able to see the template Magento uses there:

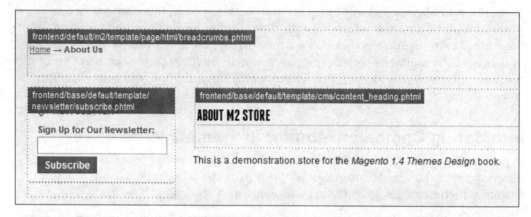

The file is called subscribe.phtml and is located in the /app/design/frontend/ base/default/template/newsletter directory. Copy-and-paste the file into your theme's templates directory (for example, /app/design/frontend/default/m2/ template/newsletter) and open the file to edit it:

```
<div class="block block-subscribe">
 <div class="block-title">
  <strong><span><?php echo $this->__('Newsletter') ?></span></strong>
 </div>
 <form action="<?php echo $this->getFormActionUrl() ?>" method="post"
id="newsletter-validate-detail">
  <div class="block-content">
   <label for="newsletter"><?php echo $this->__('Sign Up for Our
Newsletter:') ?></label>
   <div class="input-box">
    <input type="text" name="email" id="newsletter" title="<?php
echo $this->__('Sign up for our newsletter') ?>" class="input-text
required-entry validate-email" />
   </div>
   <div class="actions">
    <button type="submit" title="<?php echo $this->__('Subscribe') ?>"
class="button"><span><span><?php echo $this->__('Subscribe') ?></
span></span></button>
   </div>
```

```
    </div>
    </form>
    <script type="text/javascript">
    //<![CDATA[
    var newsletterSubscriberFormDetail = new VarienForm('newsletter-
validate-detail');
    //]]>
    </script>
    </div>
```

This allows subscription to the built-in Magento newsletter system.

Getting the Campaign Monitor subscription form markup

Log in to your Campaign Monitor control panel and select the relevant client account that you want to use for the newsletters on your Magento store, and then select the **Lists & Subscribers** tab towards the top of the screen:

In the right-hand column of the screen, you should now see the option to **Create a subscribe form**:

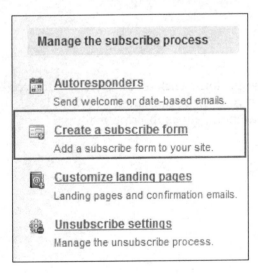

You will then be presented with options of which fields to include, that define the information you collect about the subscribers to your mailing list. Also present here is a list of mailing lists you are able to add a subscriber to; it is best to just subscribe them to one list unless you explicitly state that they will be signed up to multiple lists (for example, 'Latest products' newsletters and 'Latest discounts and offers' newsletters).

> **Collecting and using names?**
> It can be a good idea to collect a name alongside an e-mail address for your newsletter campaigns as this allows you to tailor the newsletter to your individual customer (for example, 'Dear Richard' is more friendly than 'Dear customer').

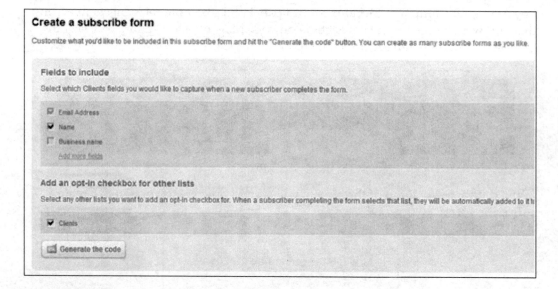

Once you've completed the form, click on the **Generate the code** button at the bottom of the form and you will be presented with the HTML that you need for your Campaign Monitor newsletter subscription form:

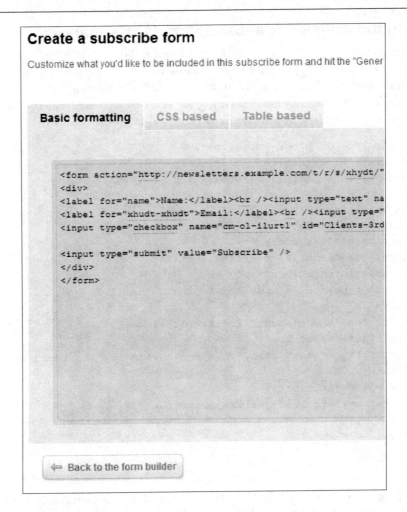

The markup generated by Campaign Monitor will look similar to the following:

```html
<form action="http://newsletters.example.com/t/r/s/xhydt/"
method="post" id="subForm">
  <div>
  <label for="name">Name:</label><br />
  <input type="text" name="cm-name" id="name" /><br />
  <label for="xhudt-xhudt">Email:</label><br />
  <input type="text" name="cm-xhudt-xhudt" id="xhudt-xhudt" /><br />
  <input type="checkbox" name="cm-ol-ilurtl" id="Clients" />
  <label for="Clients">Clients</label><br />
  <input type="submit" value="Subscribe" />
  </div>
</form>
```

Updating the newsletter subscription form's markup

Now return to the `subscribe.phtml` file and replace the content of the `<form>`
element with the following, be sure to re-include the `.block-content <div>`
element to wrap the entirety of the content of the form, removing the checkbox to
select which list the customer is subscribing to. You can also take this opportunity
to remove superfluous line break elements (`<br />`) from the markup:

```
<div class="block block-subscribe">
 <div class="block-title">
  <h3><?php echo $this->__('Newsletter') ?></h3>
 </div>
 <form action="http://newsletters.example.com/t/r/s/xhydt/"
method="post" id="subForm">
  <div class="block-content">
   <label for="name">Name:</label><br />
   <div class="input-box">
    <input type="text" name="cm-name" id="name" />
   </div>
   <label for="xhudt-xhudt">Email:</label><br />
   <div class="input-box">
    <input type="text" name="cm-xhudt-xhudt" id="xhudt-xhudt" />
   </div>
   <div class="actions">
    <input type="submit" value="Subscribe" />
   </div>
  </div>
 </form>
</div>
```

As you did before with the sidebar blocks, you can also change the title of the block
to use a `<h3>` element, so that the styling matches the other blocks in the sidebar.

Open your Magento theme's `local.xml` file (in the layout directory of your theme,
for example, `/app/design/frontend/default/m2/layout`) and add the following
lines within the `<default>` handle to display the newsletter subscribe box at the
right-hand column on all pages:

```
<default>
  <!-- other omitted layout for the default handle -->
 <reference name="right">
  <block type="newsletter/subscribe" after="-" name="right.newsletter"
template="newsletter/subscribe.phtml"/>
 </reference>
</default>
```

If you now refresh the frontend of your store, you should see the newsletter subscription block for Campaign Monitor you have just created appear in the right-hand column of your store's design (as well as the left-hand column, which you could remove through layout as explained in an earlier chapter):

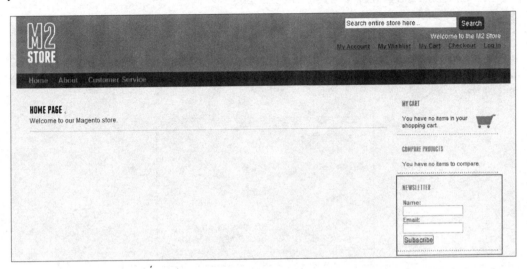

You can now apply some styles to the elements in this block as a finishing touch. Open your theme's `local.css` file in the `/skin/frontend/default/m2/css` directory and add the following lines:

```css
.block-subscribe input[type="text"] {
border: 1px #CCC solid;
width: 170px
}

/* The submit button */
.block-subscribe div.actions input {
background: #F76300;
border: none;
color: #FFF;
display: block;
font-weight: bold;
padding: 2px 5px;
text-align: center;
width: 172px
}
```

You can also make use of :hover to style the subscription button when it is hovered over to provide your visitors with an indication that they are able to interact with the element:

```
.block-subscribe div.action input:hover {
opacity: 0.6
}
```

If you now save your local.css file and refresh your Magento store's frontend, you can see that the newsletter subscription form looks more consistently styled with the rest of the store:

Making Magento e-mail templates ready for use

By default, Magento's e-mail templates do not contain information that relates to your own store; they contain dummy data. Before you start to use the e-mail templates on your 'live' store, you will need to change these instances of dummy data. You will find the files you need to change in the /app/local/en_US/ template/email directory of your Magento installation (if you're using a language or 'locale' other than en_US—that is, American English here, you will need to change this value in the directory path).

For this example, use the wishlist_share.html file. In this file, you will see an instance of the words "Demo Store", which need changing to reflect your own store's name:

```
<td valign="top">
<p>Hey,<br/>
Take a look at my wishlist from Demo Store.</p>
```

Change this to:

```
<td valign="top">
<p>Hey,<br/>
Take a look at my wishlist from M2 Store.</p>
```

Looking through other template files in this directory, you will see other instances of dummy data, including the following:

- A dummy e-mail address for your store, dummyemail@magentocommerce.com; you will also need to change instances of mailto:magento@varien.com and mailto:dummyemail@magentocommerce.com with your own store's e-mail address

- A dummy telephone number for your store, (800) DEMO-STORE

- A variation of the dummy store name from before, Magento Demo Store

- Dummy opening hours for your store, Monday - Friday, 8am - 5pm PST

Simply replace these values for values relevant for your own Magento store and the templates are ready for use on a 'live' store!

> **Sample transactional e-mail templates**
>
> If you're looking for sample transactional e-mail templates to work from, you can try the Brazilian Email Templates package available for free from http://www.magentocommerce.com/module/2722/brazilian-email-templates.

Upgrade-proof e-mail templates

There is a Magento extension that allows for upgrade-proof e-mail templates. By default, Magento e-mail templates are overwritten. The extension, **CLS Upgrade-proof Email Templates** (http://www.magentocommerce.com/magento-connect/Erik+-+Classy+Llama+Studios/extension/1416/cls-upgrade-proof-email-templates), alters Magento to allow for the e-mail templates to be overwritten in the same fallback architecture as the store's theme templates. If you insert your e-mail template files in the /app/design/frontend/your_interface/your_theme/locale/en_US /templates/email/ directory, the extension will ensure that these e-mail templates are used in place of those located in the /app/locale/en_US/templates directory (assuming your store uses the en_US locale).

Testing e-mail templates

As with your Magento store's theme, you may wish to test your newly created or changed e-mail templates before sending them to clients. You can test templates through third-party systems such as Limtus (`http://litmus.com/email-previews`), that allow you to remotely view your e-mail template on a large selection of operating systems and e-mail clients. E-mail on Acid (`http://www.emailonacid.com`) allows you to 'preview your e-mail in 48 variations of the most popular e-mail clients and mobile devices'.

Testing in Campaign Monitor

The Campaign Monitor system has a built-in testing feature for design that you can read more about at `http://www.campaignmonitor.com/testing/`. The system can also help identify any problems your e-mail template is likely to incur with e-mail programs and webmail spam filters.

Summary

In this chapter, you have looked at transactional e-mail and newsletter templates within Magento, and into specific third-party e-mail newsletter systems that you can integrate with Magento.

In particular, you've seen how to edit transactional e-mail templates in your store. Along with customizing templates for Magento's own newsletter system. You also integrated popular e-mail newsletter systems in your Magento theme: Campaign Monitor.

We made Magento's e-mail templates ready for use and tested the e-mail templates too.

In the coming chapters, you will begin to integrate social media features from Twitter and Facebook into your store and style your store for printing too.

Social Media and Magento

9

With the emerging popularity of the 'social web', it is becoming more and more common to integrate aspects from social media tools such as Twitter and Facebook into e-commerce stores, such as those powered by the Magento platform. Social media can provide a fantastic opportunity for e-commerce store owners to participate and engage with existing and potential customers while increasing the awareness of their products among a wider audience. This chapter covers integrating your Magento store:

- With Twitter, including:
    - Adding a 'Follow Us On Twitter' button
    - Making use of the Twitter 'latest tweets' widgets to your store

- With Facebook, comprising of how to:
    - Add a Facebook 'Like' button to your product detail pages to help spread the word about your products
    - Make use of the Facebook widget to include the latest changes to your Facebook page

Twitter integration with Magento

Twitter (http://twitter.com) is a social network that lets its users follow others
and read short messages (tweets) sent by them; it is a micro-blogging system.

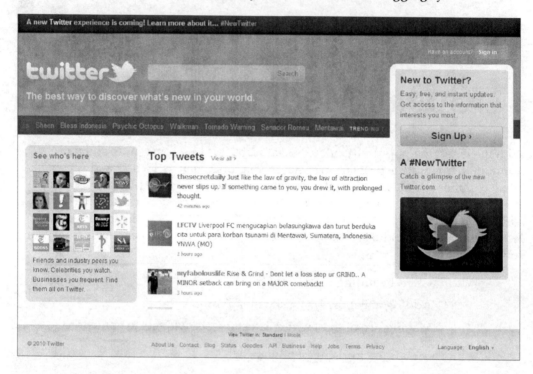

You will need to create a Twitter account or log in to your store's existing Twitter
account to follow the next steps.

Adding a 'Follow Us On Twitter' button to your Magento store

One of the more simple ways to integrate your store's Twitter feed with Magento is
to add a 'Follow Us On Twitter' button to your store's design.

Generating the markup from the Twitter website

Go to the Twitter Goodies website (http://twitter.com/about/resources):

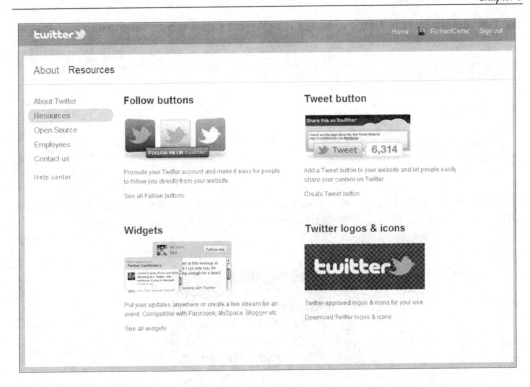

Select the **Follow Buttons** option and then select the **Looking for Follow us on Twitter buttons?** towards the bottom of the screen:

The buttons will now change to the **FOLLOW US ON Twitter** buttons:

Select the style of button you'd like to make use of on your Magento store and then select the generated HTML that is provided in the pop-up that is displayed:

The generated HTML for the M2 Store's Twitter account (with the username of **M2MagentoStore**) looks like the following:

```
<a href="http://www.twitter.com/M2MagentoStore">
  <img src="http://twitter-badges.s3.amazonaws.com/follow_us-a.png"
alt="Follow M2MagentoStore on Twitter"/>
</a>
```

Adding a static block in Magento for your Twitter button

Now you will need to create a new static block in the Magento CMS feature: navigate to **CMS | Static Blocks** in your Magento store's administration panel and click on **Add New Block**.

As you did when creating a static block for the supplier logos used in your store's footer, complete the form to create the new static block. Add the **Follow Us On Twitter** button to the **Content** field by disabling the Rich Text Editor with the **Show/Hide Editor** button and pasting in the markup you generated previously:

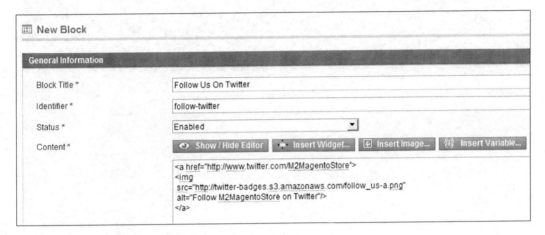

 You don't need to upload an image to your store through Magento's CMS here as the Twitter buttons are hosted elsewhere.

Note that the **Identifier** field reads **follow-twitter**—you will need this for the layout changes you are about to make!

Updating your theme's layout file for the 'Follow Us' button

Open your theme's `local.xml` file in its `/layout` directory (for example, `/app/design/frontend/default/m2/layout`) and locate the `<default>` handle in your store, inserting the following XML to add the new static block to the right-hand column (`name="right"`)

```
<reference name="right">
 <block type="cms/block" name="follow-twitter" after="-">
  <action method="setBlockId">
   <block_id>follow-twitter</block_id>
  </action>
 </block>
</reference>
```

Save and upload your `local.xml` file, and then refresh the frontend of your Magento store and you will see your new **FOLLOW US ON Twitter** button appear in your theme:

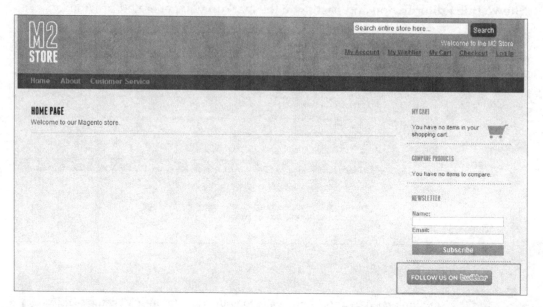

Embedding a 'latest tweets' widget into your Magento store

You may prefer to directly embed your store's messages from Twitter into your store. Return to the Twitter Resources page (`http://twitter.com/about/resources`) and select the **Widgets** option this time. From the tabs on the left-hand side of the screen, select the **My Website** option and you will then be presented with a list of Twitter widgets you can use on your store:

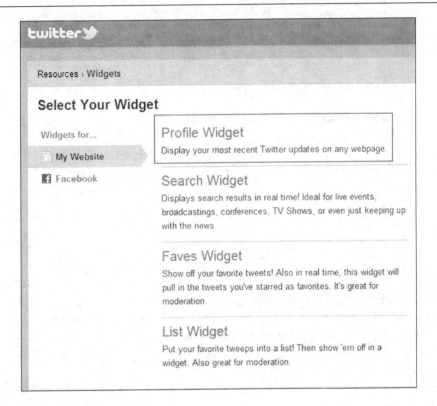

Select the **Profile Widget** option at the top and you will then need to type the Twitter account's username into the **Username** field presented if it is not already populated. You can also style the widget through the tabs along the left-hand side of the screen. In particular you will want to customize the **Dimensions** settings so that the widget fits in the column of your Magento store's theme (a value of around 180px here works well):

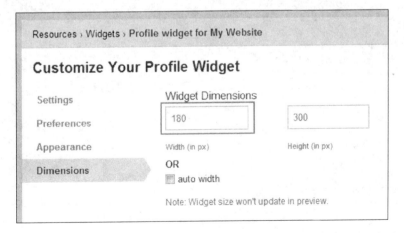

Once you've finished, click on the **Finish & Grab Code** button at the bottom of the screen:

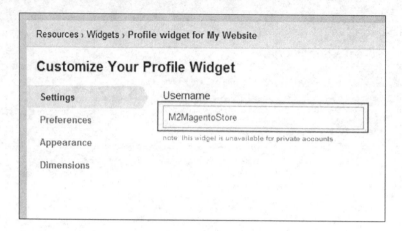

Copy the HTML generated by Twitter for your widget at this point and log in to your Magento administration panel. The HTML generated is all within `<script>` elements and should look similar to the following:

```
<script src="http://widgets.twimg.com/j/2/widget.js"></script>
<script>
new TWTR.Widget({
  version: 2,
  type: 'profile',
  rpp: 5,
  interval: 6000,
  width: 180,
  height: 300,
  theme: {
    shell: {
      background: '#f76300',
      color: '#ffffff'
    },
    tweets: {
      background: '#f76300',
      color: '#ffffff',
      links: '#a04000'
    }
  },
  features: {
    scrollbar: true,
    loop: false,
    live: false,
    hashtags: true,
    timestamp: true,
```

```
        avatars: false,
        behavior: 'all'
    }
}).render().setUser('M2MagentoStore').start();
</script>
```

 The last line inside the second `<script>` element is where your Twitter username is defined, so you can change the value here if you ever move Twitter accounts!

Return to Magento's CMS feature and create another static block in **CMS | Static Blocks** by clicking on the **Add New Block** button, and filling the **Block Title**, **Identifier**, and **Status** fields with suitable values (note that the **Identifier** value is **widget-twitter** here as you'll need this soon):

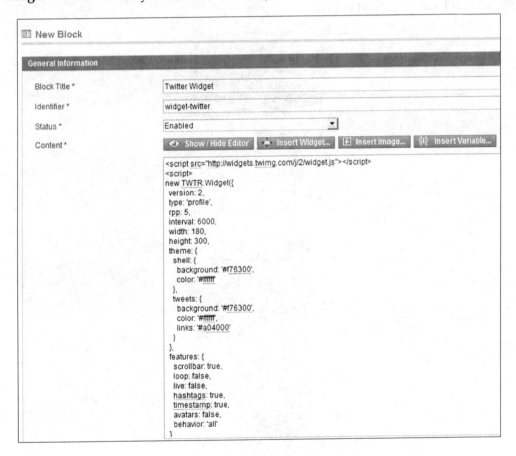

Click on **Save Block** at the top-right of your screen and then open your theme's `local.xml` file (in the `/app/design/frontend/default/m2/layout` directory) for editing. Within the `<default>` handle, you can insert the following layout to add your latest tweets to the left-hand column of your store:

```
<reference name="left">
 <block type="cms/block" name="widget-twitter" after="-">
  <action method="setBlockId">
   <block_id>widget-twitter</block_id>
  </action>
 </block>
</reference>
```

The Twitter widget will now appear in your store's left-hand column (for example, your store's **About** page may still have a left-hand column), below any other content blocks you have displayed in it:

You could change the position of the widget's block within the column by altering `after="-"` to `before="-"`.

Integrating Twitter through Magento extensions

There are a number of extensions that you can use to integrate Twitter into your Magento store's theme with less effort than the methods seen previously, but they tend to be more restrictive as to where you can use them or in how they function within Magento.

Name of extension	Description of extension
Magentweet http://www.magentweet.com	Magentweet allows you to embed Twitter in your store's CMS pages and can be configured to show either tweets from a specified Twitter account or real-time search results for a specific phrase or 'hashtag'.
Twitter Tweet Button http://www.magentocommerce.com/magento-connect/C3+Media/extension/4446/c3_tweetbutton	The Twitter Tweet Button extension for Magento allows you to add a button to various pages in your store (such as the store's homepage, CMS pages, category pages, product pages) which then allows your store's visitor to tweet the page of the store that they are currently viewing. This extension is fairly configurable, with options to configure the styling of the button, the language it appears in and for you to manually set the URL, and message that is to be tweeted.
Share Tweet http://www.magentocommerce.com/magento-connect/prateek+gupta./extension/3862/share_tweet	Share Tweet is a paid extension for Twitter which provides integration with Magento to allow your customers to share their thoughts about products and pages on your store. The extension supports the OAuth method of authentication with Twitter and is configurable.
VK_TwitterPL http://www.magentocommerce.com/magento-connect/vivek291186/extension/4956/vk_twitterpl	The VK_TwitterPL extension for Magento allows you to embed the latest tweets from a specified Twitter account into your Magento store but is less configurable than other extensions such as Magentweet.

Name of extension	Description of extension

Mage SlideTweet
 	
`http://www.`
`magentocommerce.com/`
`magento-connect/`
`webkul/extension/5015/`
`mage_slidetweet`
	The Mage SlideTweet extension for Magento is a paid extension, that displays tweets that slide in and out. The extension is highly configurable with the width, height, and color of the widget being definable, and you are also able to configure the speed at which new tweets slide into the page.
	
	The extension is embedded by making use of the 'embed widget' tool in Magento's content editor.

Meanbee Promote/Share Order
 	
`http://www.`
`magentocommerce.com/`
`magento-connect/`
`Meanbee/extension/4103/`
`meanbee_ordershare`
	The Meanbee Promote/Share Order extension for Magento adds a 'tweet this' button to your store's order success page, enabling your customers to tweet once they've placed an order through your store.
	
	This extension also provides a Facebook 'Like' button with similar functionality.

Magento on Twitter

The Magento project has its own Twitter account at `http://twitter.com/magento`.

Integrating Facebook with Magento

Facebook (`http://www.facebook.com`) is a social networking website that allows people to add each other as 'friends' and to send messages and share content.

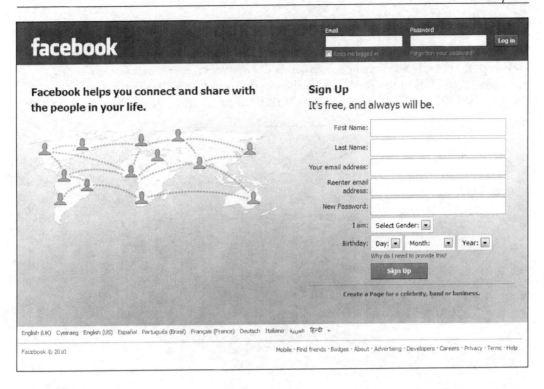

As with Twitter, there are two options you have for integrating Facebook with your Magento store:

1. Adding a 'Like' button to your store's product pages to allow your customers to show their appreciation for individual products on your store.

2. Integrating a widget of the latest news from your store's Facebook profile.

Adding a 'Like' button to your Magento store's product pages

The Facebook 'Like' button allows Facebook users to show that they approve of a particular web page and you can put this to use on your Magento store.

Getting the 'Like' button markup

To get the markup required for your store's 'Like' button, go to the Facebook Developers website at: http://developers.facebook.com/docs/reference/plugins/like. Fill in the form below the description text with relevant values, leaving the **URL to like** field as **URLTOLIKE** for now, and setting the **Width** to **200**:

Click on the **Get Code** button at the bottom of the form and then copy the code that is presented in the **iframe** field:

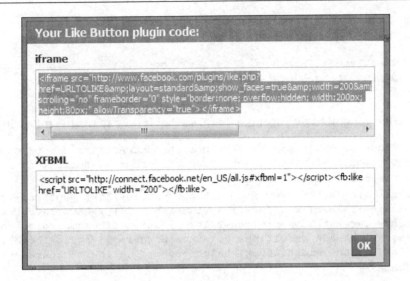

The generated markup should look like the following:

```
<iframe  src="http://www.facebook.com/plugins/like.php?href=URLTOLIKE&
amp;layout=standard&amp;show_faces=true&amp;width=200&amp;action=like&
amp;colorscheme=light&amp;height=80"
 scrolling="no" frameborder="0"
 style="border:none; overflow:hidden; width:200px; height:80px;"
allowTransparency="true">
</iframe>
```

You now need to replace the **URLTOLIKE** in the previous markup to the URL of the current page in your Magento store. The PHP required to do this in Magento looks like the following:

```
<?php
 $currentUrl = $this->helper('core/url')->getCurrentUrl();
?>
```

The new **Like** button markup for your Magento store should now look like the following:

```
<iframe src="http://www.facebook.com/plugins/like.php?href=
".<?php $currentUrl = $this->helper('core/url')->getCurrentUrl();
?>".
&amp;layout=standard&amp;show_faces=true&amp;width=200&amp;action=like
&amp;colorscheme=light&amp;height=80»
 scrolling="no" frameborder="0"
 style="border:none; overflow:hidden; width:200px; height:80px;"
allowTransparency="true">
</iframe>
```

Open your theme's `view.phtml` file in the `/app/design/frontend/default/m2/template/catalog/product` directory and locate the lines that read:

```
<div class="std"><?php echo $_helper->productAttribute($_product,
nl2br($_product->getShortDescription()), 'short_description') ?></div>
</div>
```

Insert the code generated by Facebook here, so that it now reads the following:

```
<div class="std"><?php echo $_helper->productAttribute($_product,
nl2br($_product->getShortDescription()), 'short_description') ?></div>
 <!-- Chapter 9: Like button -->
 <iframe  src="http://www.facebook.com/plugins/like.php?href=<?php
echo $this->helper('core/url')->getCurrentUrl();?>&amp;layout=standard
&amp;show_faces=true&amp;width=200&amp;action=like&amp;colorscheme=li
ght&amp;height=80" scrolling="no" frameborder="0" style="border:none;
overflow:hidden; width:200px; height:80px;"  allowTransparency="true">
 </iframe>
</div>
```

Save and upload this file back to your Magento installation and then visit a product page within your store to see the button appear below the brief description of the product:

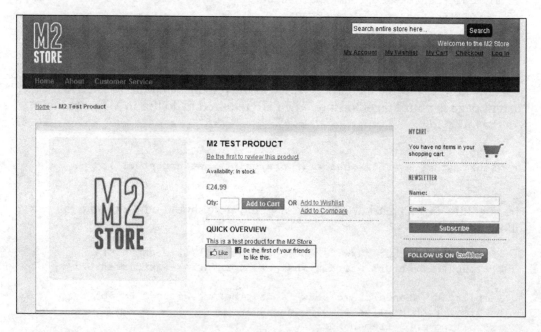

That's it, your product pages can now be liked on Facebook!

Integrating the Facebook 'Like box' widget in your Magento store

As with Twitter, Facebook also provides a widget which you can embed in your Magento store to display recent posts and content you have posted to your Facebook page's profile.

Navigate to the Facebook Developer page for plugins (`http://developers.facebook.com/plugins`) and select the **Like box** option. Similarly to the **Like** button markup generator for Facebook, you are presented with a form you need to complete to generate the necessary markup:

Click on the **Get Code** button at the bottom and then, once again, copy the generated markup from the **iframe** panel presented:

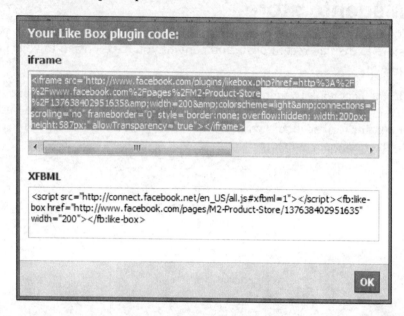

The markup generated for the Facebook **Like box** you're embedding in your Magento store should look similar to the following:

```
<iframe src="http://www.facebook.com/plugins/likebox.
php?href=http%3A%2F%2Fwww.facebook.com%2Fpages%2FM2-Product-Store%2F13
7638402951635&amp;width=200&amp;colorscheme=light&amp;connections=10&a
mp;stream=true&amp;header=true&amp;height=587"
scrolling="no" frameborder="0"
style="border:none; overflow:hidden; width:200px; height:587px;"
allowTransparency="true">
</iframe>
```

Go to your Magento store's administration panel and navigate to **CMS | Static Blocks**. Create a new static block in your store by clicking **Add New Block** to the top-right of your screen, and complete the fields as before. When you come to the **Content** field, paste the code generated from Facebook into the field after you have disabled the Rich Text Editor by clicking the **Show/Hide Editor** button:

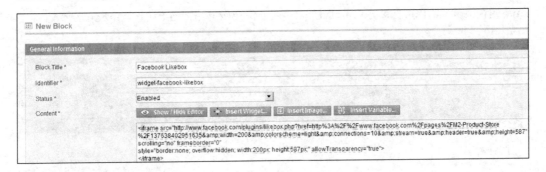

Note that the **Identifier** field has the value **widget-facebook-likebox**, as you will need this for the consequent layout changes you need to make to Magento. Click on the **Save Block** button at the top-right of your screen to store the new static block in your Magento store.

Open your Magento theme's `local.xml` file (for example, in the `/app/design/ frontend/default/m2/layout` directory) and create a new layout handle called `<cms_index_index>` within the `<layout>` elements:

```
<cms_index_index>
 <reference name="right">
  <block type="cms/block" name="widget-facebook-likebox" after="-">
   <action method="setBlockId">
      <block_id>widget-facebook-likebox</block_id>
   </action>
  </block>
 </reference>
</cms_index_index>
```

Save and upload this file to your Magento installation and refresh your store's frontend view:

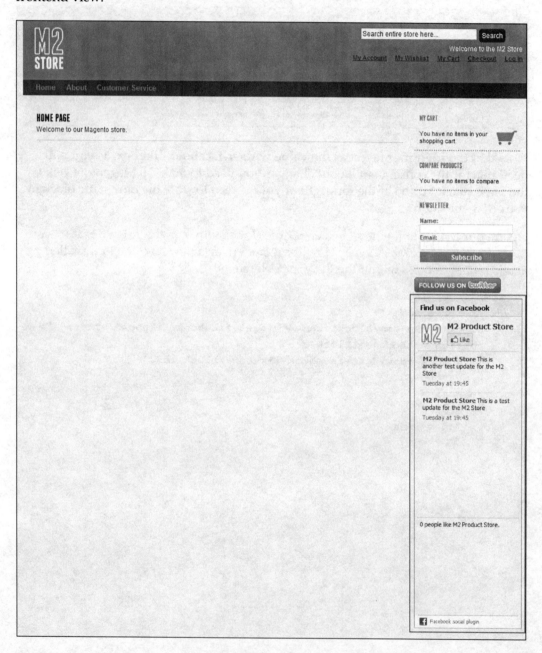

> **Can't see the Like box?**
>
> The `<cms_index_index>` handle means that the Facebook Like box will only be visible on your store's homepage.

Integrating Facebook with Magento extensions

As with Twitter, it is also possible to integrate Facebook into your Magento store with the use of extensions from the Magento Community.

Name of extension	Description of extension
Beeshoppy http://www.magentocommerce.com/magento-connect/Beecoder/extension/3659/beecoder_beeshopy	The Beeshoppy extension allows you to embed your Magento store into Facebook. While the extension is free, you will need to create an account at http://www.beeshopy.com to use this extension.
Meanbee Promote/Share Order http://www.magentocommerce.com/magento-connect/Meanbee/extension/4103/meanbee_ordershare	The Meanbee Promote/Share Order extension for Magento adds Facebook's **Like** button to your store's order success page, enabling your customers to tell their Facebook friends once they've placed an order through your store. This extension also provides a Twitter 'tweet this' button with similar functionality.
Facebook Like Button http://www.magentocommerce.com/magento-connect/TemplatesMaster/extension/3816/facebooklb	The Facebook Like Button extension for Magento adds a Facebook **Like** button beneath your product's title on the product detail pages of your store.
Facebook Connect Social Shopping http://www.magentocommerce.com/magento-connect/Optaros%2C+Inc/extension/1970/facebook-connect-social-shopping	The Facebook Connect Social Shopping extension provides an embedded chat feature that allows your customers to ask friends' opinions on products in your store.

Further social media integration with Magento

There are other options available to you if you are looking to integrate your Magento store with social media.

Social bookmarking in Magento

Social bookmarking tools allow users to save their bookmarks in a central space on the Internet, meaning that they are accessible from anywhere with Internet access, and making social bookmarks more convenient than traditional browser-based bookmarks.

ShareThisProduct extension for Twitter, Facebook, and MySpace

If you are looking to make use of Twitter, Facebook, and MySpace in your Magento store, you may find the ShareThisProduct extension for Magento available at: `http://www.magentocommerce.com/magento-connect/herve%40wsa/extension/4802/sharethisproduct`, useful. The extension adds links to your store's product details view for the page to be shared on the Twitter, Facebook, and MySpace social networks.

Magento Social Bookmarking Services extension

The Magento Social Bookmarking Services extension provides similar functionality to the previous ShareThisProduct extension for Magento, but allows for more configuration as to where the widget containing the social bookmarking buttons appears in your store.

You can find the extension at `http://www.magentocommerce.com/magento-connect/_Fluxe/extension/2333/magento-social-bookmarking`.

Logging in with a social networking account

Many people have an account with a social network such as Twitter or Facebook these days and registering a new account can be off-putting for some customers. There is, however, an extension that enables customers using the more popular social networks and even the PayPal payment gateway to log in to your Magento store. The extension is called Engage (`http://www.magentocommerce.com/magento-connect/GothicJB/extension/4946/engage`).

As mentioned, the benefit of such an extension is that your customers do not need to create a separate account to buy from your store, which may lead to increased conversions and sales in your Magento store.

Summary

In this chapter, you have explored various methods of integrating social media from Twitter and Facebook into your Magento store including adding a **Follow Us On Twitter** button to your store and embedding a Twitter 'latest tweets' widget. We also added a Facebook **Like** button to your product pages and made use of the Facebook widget to include the latest news from your Magento store's Facebook page.

The next chapter styles your Magento store for print.

10
Magento Print Style

Your Magento store can list hundreds, even thousands of products online, accessible through web browsers. You've styled your store for the web but what about when a section of it is printed? This chapter delves into styling your Magento store pages for printing, including the following:

- What the Default Magento theme already does to style items for printing
- Using Magento layout to include a print stylesheet
- Creating a theme-specific print stylesheet
- Overcoming a common browser-specific problem in the print stylesheets

Magento Default theme's print styling

As you might expect given the hierarchy of themes in Magento, some print styling has already been done for you. If you use a tool such as Firefox's Web Developer extension (`http://chrispederick.com/work/web-developer/`), you can view the effect this CSS has on the page's appearance by selecting **CSS | Display CSS By Media Type | Print** in the toolbar the extension adds in Firefox:

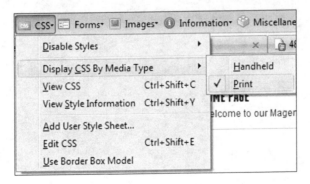

As you can see the default screen styling makes extensive use of background colors in large quantities to distinguish between the various visual areas of your store: the header, the footer, and the content blocks in particular:

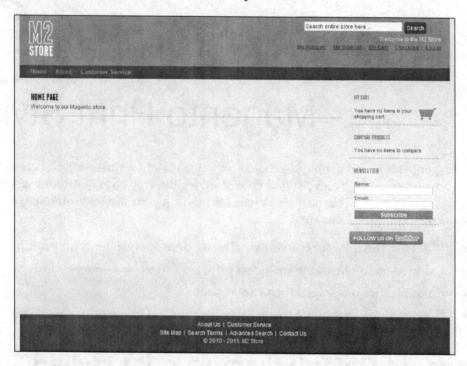

You can see that the print style in Magento defines some rules for hiding the header and footer areas of your store, and resetting colors in certain elements such as `<body>` to display as black text on a white background, which is ideal for printing:

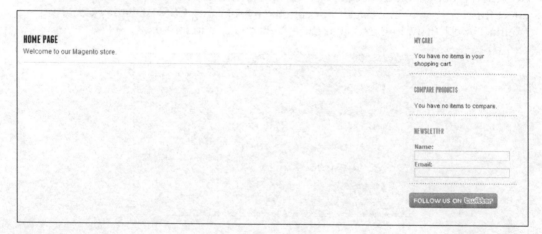

If you look in the `<head>` element of your store's source code, you should see the following line:

```
<link rel="stylesheet"
type="text/css" href="http://www.example.com//magento/skin/frontend/
default/default/css/print.css" media="print"
/>
```

Looking at this `print.css` file, you should see that the following CSS is given for your Magento store. Firstly, the colors in various elements are reset to more print-friendly values:

```
* {
background:none !important;
text-align:left !important;
}
html {
margin:0 !important;
padding:0 !important;
}
body {
background:#fff !important;
font-size:9pt !important;
padding:0 !important;
margin:10px !important;
}
a {
color:#2976c9 !important;
}
th,td {
color:#2f2f2f !important;
border-color:#ccc !important;
}
```

Secondly, the header and footer areas are hidden, as navigational elements are unnecessary in a print version of your store, as the visitors would be unable to interact with them:

```
.header-container,
.nav-container,
.footer-container,
.pager,
.toolbar,
.actions,
.buttons-set {
display:none !important;
}
```

Lastly, two small changes are made to fix styling for the cart view in your
Magento store:

```
.page-print .data-table .cart-tax-total {
background-position:100% -54px;
}
.page-print .data-table .cart-tax-info {
display:block !important;
}
```

It is also worthwhile looking at the current styling of the product detail view in
your Magento theme too, as customers are reasonably likely to want to print these
to show friends or family members before making a decision about buying your
products. If you recall, your theme's product detail page will currently look similar
to the following:

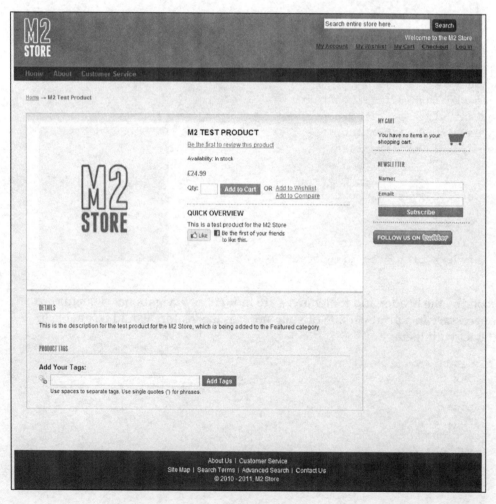

As with the print styling of your Magento store's homepage earlier in this chapter, the header and footer elements of the store are hidden here:

There are still some elements that you can see that require hiding for print styling. In particular:

- The entirety of the right-hand column can be hidden, as it requires no useful information that someone reading the printed version of your store would be able to use or interact with. This is especially true for the **Newsletter** form.

- Within the product details, there are many elements you can hide, such as the following:
  - The **Be the first to review this product** link.
  - The **Qty** (quantity) fields.
  - The Facebook 'Like' button you embedded in the previous chapter (which has produced errors).
  - The **PRODUCT TAGS** section.

You will look into creating a customized print stylesheet for your Magento 1.4 store shortly, but first it is important to know of factors you should consider when creating your print stylesheet.

Using Magento layout to include a print stylesheet

Your first task in creating a print stylesheet for your Magento theme is to use Magento layout to tell Magento to include your new stylesheet. Open your theme's `local.xml` file (in the `/app/design/frontend/default/m2/layout` directory) and locate the `<default>` handle. Using an `addCss` action in Magento layout, add the following to your theme's `local.xml` layout file, which will reference the file in the `<head>` element of every page within your Magento store:

```
<reference name="head">
 <action method="addCss">
  <stylesheet>css/m2-print.css</stylesheet>
  <params>media="print"</params>
 </action>
</reference>
```

The print stylesheet you want to include in your Magento theme is called `m2-print.css`, that you'll create next. Once you have uploaded the file again, look at the source of your Magento store and confirm that you can see the following line within the `<head>` element of your store:

```
<link
 rel="stylesheet"
 type="text/css"
href="http://www.example.com/magento/skin/frontend/base/default/css/
m2-print.css"
 media="print"
 />
```

You've now successfully used Magento XML layout to add a print stylesheet to your Magento theme.

Magento theme hierarchy in action

Notice that, as you are yet to create the `m2-print.css` file in your theme's `/css` directory, Magento's theme hierarchy system defaults to looking in the Base interface's Default theme (`/base/default`) as a last resort to finding the `m2-print.css` file.

Your next step is adding the necessary CSS to your new print stylesheet.

Customizing the Magento administration panel for print

In the course of administering your Magento store, you may find that it's useful to add a 'print label' feature to your store's administration panel, this creates a pop-up of a label you can print and apply to your dispatched packages. A guide to doing this is available on the Magento Wiki at http://www.magentocommerce.com/wiki/4_-_themes_ and_template_customization/checkout/print_labels.

Creating a custom print stylesheet for your Magento theme

As you will doubtlessly have noticed by now, a good print stylesheet for your store needs to do at least two things:

1. Hide any unnecessary or useless content: this is especially true of elements in your store that a customer could usually interact with on their screen (for example, navigational links and forms).

2. Restyle the remaining elements to be more suitable for print, especially in terms of the colors used.

You can continue to customize the print view of your Magento store by creating a new CSS file called m2-print.css and saving it in your theme's /skin/frontend/ default/m2/css directory. Open this file for editing, and begin adding custom CSS rules to hide and style the relevant elements of your Magento store.

Print style for content blocks in Magento

Firstly, use CSS to hide the right-hand and left-hand columns in the store:

```
.col-right,
.col-left {
display: none
}
```

It's also a good idea to stretch the content <div> to 100% width so that it fills the page when printed:

```
.col-main {
float: none;
width: 100%
}
```

If you now save and upload the changes you've made so far, you'll see the effect this has had on the print view of your store:

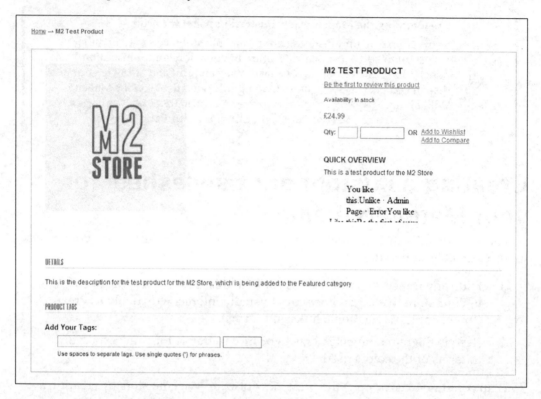

Next, you can remove the **Be the first to review this product** feature from the store. A brief look at this page's source code reveals that it is contained within a paragraph element with class `.no-rating`:

```
<p class="no-rating">
 <a href="http://www.example.com/magento/index.php/review/product/
list/id/1/#review-form">
  Be the first to review this product
 </a>
</p>
```

As such, you can simply add to your `m2-print.css` file to hide this element:

```
.col-right,
.col-left,
.no-rating {
display: none
}
```

After refreshing the frontend of your Magento store, you should see the ratings block disappear from the view:

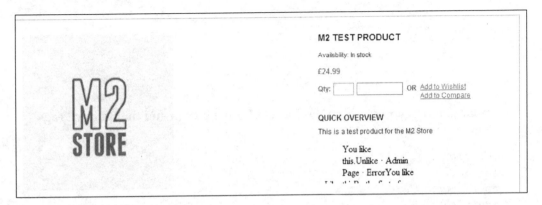

The next element you can style for your store's print view are the **Qty** (quantity) fields, displayed below the price field (**£24.99** in the preceding screenshot):

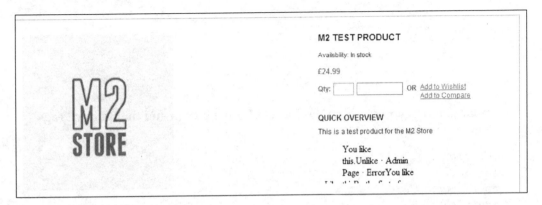

Another brief view of the page's source code reveals that these elements are contained within a `<div>` of class `.add-to-box`, so you can add to your print stylesheet to remove this element, too:

```
.col-right,
.col-left,
.no-rating,
.add-to-box {
display: none
}
```

After refreshing the page once again after you have saved and uploaded this change, this element will have disappeared from your store's print view:

M2 TEST PRODUCT

Availability: In stock

£24.99

QUICK OVERVIEW

This is a test product for the M2 Store

In a similar manner, you can hide the Facebook **Like** button and the **Product Tags** feature from your store's print view:

```
.col-right,
.col-left,
.no-rating,
.add-to-box,
iframe,
.box-tags {
display: none
}
```

The styling of your store's print view is now more complete, with the majority of the unnecessary and or unwanted elements being hidden from view for customers who do decide to print content from your store:

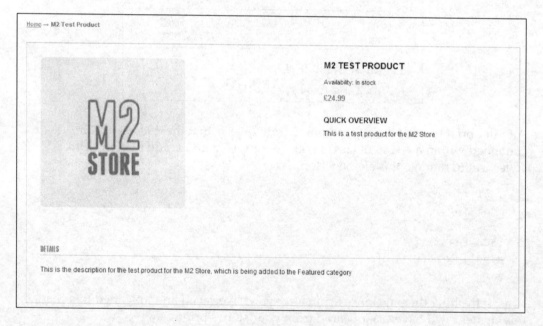

If you check your store's homepage, you'll see that the columns have been removed by the new print stylesheet too:

HOME PAGE
Welcome to our Magento store.

Print style for typography in Magento

Another aspect of your Magento theme's print stylesheet that you may want to change is the typography: by default, the store's stylesheets use sans-serif typefaces that are generally easier to read on screen but not as easy to read once printed.

Open your theme's m2-print.css file again and define a suitable font-family attribute. It can be worth applying a slightly different, complementary typeface to the headings within the page to help them stand out against the style of the other content in the page, and to redefine the hierarchy of sizes for headings within the page to distinguish between each type of heading:

```
body {
font-family: "times", "times new roman", "georgia", serif;
font-size: 13pt;
line-height: 1.35em
}
h1,h2,h3,h4,h5,h6 {
font-family: "baskerville old face", "georgia", serif
}
h1 {
border-bottom: 1px #666 solid;
font-size: 36pt
}
h2 {
font-size: 32pt
}
h3 {
font-size: 24pt
}
h4 {
font-size: 20pt
}
h5 {
color: #333;
font-size: 16pt
}
```

```
h6 {
color: #666;
font-size: 12pt
}
```

Look again at the print-style view for your Magento store and you should see that the font in use is a `serif` one which is more suitable for printing:

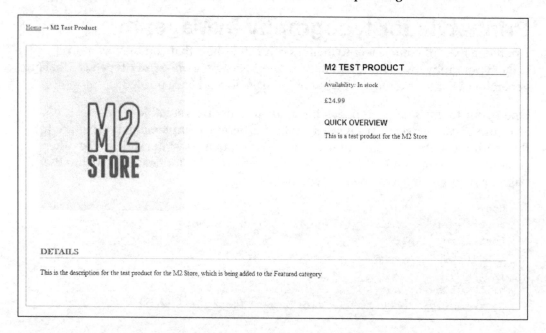

Note that the product's title (**M2 TEST PRODUCT**) still appears in the `serif` font: you can change this by adding the following line to the CSS you just defined in `m2-print.css`:

```
.product-name h1 {
font-family: "times", "times new roman", "georgia", serif !important;
}
```

If you again refresh your store's frontend in print view, you will see the styling of the product's name changed:

M2 TEST PRODUCT

Availability: In stock

£24.99

QUICK OVERVIEW

This is a test product for the M2 Store

Print style for links in Magento

You have removed most links with previous styles defined in your Magento theme's print stylesheet, but there are occasions where it would help customers if links were printed in the page. There are two problems to overcome here:

1. The links need to be stylistically distinguished from other content in your store.
2. Printed links will not display their destination (that is, `href` attribute).

Styling links

Links need to be distinguished from the remainder of the textual content in the page, for which you can define some basic CSS to embolden the link, underline it, and change the color to a familiar blue:

```
a, a:active, a:link, a:visited {
color: #09C !important;
font-weight: bold !important;
text-decoration: underline !important;
}
```

To see this style applied to your page, you may need to add a link to the content through your Magento administration panel.

Save this CSS in your theme's custom print stylesheet (for example, `m2-print.css`) and refresh the print view of the store to see the new styling applied to any link elements in the page:

DETAILS

This is the description for the test product for the M2 Store, which is being added to the Featured category.

Follow us on Twitter for more information

Displaying a printed link's destination

The next thing you need to do is display to your customers who will print pages out the destination of any links in the page. You can add this feature to your store for customers who use more modern browsers with the use of CSS added to your `m2-print.css` file:

```
a:link:after, a:visited:after {
content: " [" attr(href) "] "
}
```

The preceding CSS appends the `href` attribute in the `<a>` element to the end of a link within the page:

DETAILS

This is the description for the test product for the M2 Store, which is being added to the Featured category.

Follow us on Twitter for more information [http://www.twitter.com/M2MagentoStore]

You can also account for relative links within your store. For example, consider what would happen if you link to a page in your store as follows:

```
<a href="this-is-a-link-to-a-page">This is a link</a>
```

The current CSS would append just the value in the `href` attribute to the end of the link:

This is a link [this-is-a-link-to-a-page]

Obviously, this isn't particularly helpful to a customer who has printed this page from your website and has now forgotten your URL, so you can also add the following CSS:

```
a[href^="/"]:after {
content: " [http://www.example.com/" attr(href) "] "
}
```

This will result in the link's `href` attribute being displayed as `http://www.example.com/this-is-a-link-to-a-page`, which is much more helpful for your customers:

This is a link [http://www.example.com/this-is-a-link-to-a-page]

Don't forget to change `www.example.com` to the address of your website!

Overcoming a common browser-specific problem in print stylesheets

Finally for your print stylesheet, there is one common problem that blights some Gecko-based browsers. If content that is to be printed is contained within a long, single `<div>` element, and this element has style defined for it that applies a value for `float` other than `float: none`, any content in this element that does not fit on to the first page is not printed.

To mitigate this flaw in your print stylesheets, it is wise to ensure that any element containing `<div>`s in your Magento store have CSS defined in your theme's print stylesheet resetting the value of `float` to `float: none`.

Summary

In this chapter, you saw how to customize your Magento store for customers wanting to print pages from your store. In particular, you've learnt what the Default Magento theme already does for you and how to use Magento that is Magento's layout to include a print stylesheet in your theme.

You also learnt the basics of creating a theme-specific print stylesheet and how to mitigate a common browser-specific problem in print stylesheets.

Index

U

upgrade-proof e-mail templates 229

V

VK_TwitterPL
  about 241
  URL 241

W

WOFF (Web Open Font Format) 156

X

XML
  about 108
  elements, closing 109
  entity escapes 109
  self-closing elements 109
XML handle
  catalog_category_default 120
  catalog_product_view 120
  checkout_cart_index 120
  cms_index_defaultindex 120
  cms_index_defaultnoroute 120
  cms_page 120
  customer_account 120

Z

Zhu Zhu, Magento themes demo
  about 24, 26
  URL 24

Thank you for buying
Magento 1.4 Themes Design

About Packt Publishing

Packt, pronounced 'packed', published its first book "*Mastering phpMyAdmin for Effective MySQL Management*" in April 2004 and subsequently continued to specialize in publishing highly focused books on specific technologies and solutions.

Our books and publications share the experiences of your fellow IT professionals in adapting and customizing today's systems, applications, and frameworks. Our solution based books give you the knowledge and power to customize the software and technologies you're using to get the job done. Packt books are more specific and less general than the IT books you have seen in the past. Our unique business model allows us to bring you more focused information, giving you more of what you need to know, and less of what you don't.

Packt is a modern, yet unique publishing company, which focuses on producing quality, cutting-edge books for communities of developers, administrators, and newbies alike. For more information, please visit our website: www.packtpub.com.

About Packt Open Source

In 2010, Packt launched two new brands, Packt Open Source and Packt Enterprise, in order to continue its focus on specialization. This book is part of the Packt Open Source brand, home to books published on software built around Open Source licences, and offering information to anybody from advanced developers to budding web designers. The Open Source brand also runs Packt's Open Source Royalty Scheme, by which Packt gives a royalty to each Open Source project about whose software a book is sold.

Writing for Packt

We welcome all inquiries from people who are interested in authoring. Book proposals should be sent to author@packtpub.com. If your book idea is still at an early stage and you would like to discuss it first before writing a formal book proposal, contact us; one of our commissioning editors will get in touch with you.

We're not just looking for published authors; if you have strong technical skills but no writing experience, our experienced editors can help you develop a writing career, or simply get some additional reward for your expertise.

Magento 1.4 Development Cookbook

ISBN: 978-1-84951-144-5 Paperback: 268 pages

A practical guide to take your Magento store to the next level by developing powerful modules and extensions

1. Develop Modules and Extensions for Magento 1.4 using PHP with ease

2. Socialize your store by writing custom modules and widgets to drive in more customers

3. Achieve a tremendous performance boost by applying powerful techniques such as YSlow, PageSpeed, and Siege

Magento: Beginner's Guide

ISBN: 978-1-847195-94-4 Paperback: 300 pages

Create a dynamic, fully featured, online store with the most powerful open source e-commerce software

1. Step-by-step guide to building your own online store

2. Focuses on the key features of Magento that you must know to get your store up and running

3. Customize the store's appearance to make it uniquely yours

4. Clearly illustrated with screenshots and a working example

Please check **www.PacktPub.com** for information on our titles

Lightning Source UK Ltd.
Milton Keynes UK
UKOW041126030112

184669UK00001B/31/P